MISSION SUSTAINABLE INDIA

MISSION SUSTAINABLE INDIA

GRIHA SHIKSHA KENDRA

ZORBA BOOKS

ZORBA BOOKS

Published by Zorba Books, June 2022

Website: www.zorbabooks.com
Email: info@zorbabooks.com

Title:- Mission Sustainable India

Printbook ISBN :- 978-93-93029-03-4
Ebook ISBN :- 978-93-93029-10-2

Zorba Books Pvt. Ltd. (opc)
Sushant Arcade,
Next to Courtyard Marriot,
Sushant Lok 1, Gurgaon – 122009, India

Printed By Thomson Press (India) Ltd. B-315, Okhla Industrial Area,
Phase 1, New Delhi- 110020

A Vision Document on

Mission Sustainable India

(Volume-2 of 4)

A Vision Document-

Conceived, Coordinated and Compiled By:

Sunil Sood

Email: sunilsolar@yahoo.co.in Mobile: 7739802112

In collaboration with:

Arvind Rastogi

Dhananjay S.Kulkarni

The Volume-2 of Vision Document on "Mission Sustainable India" has been published with the financial contributions from the following organisations and individuals:

A. List of Organisations:

1. Indian Association of Energy Management Professionals (www.iaemp.in)
2. Bhumitra, Guntur
3. M/s Technovations, Bhilai

B. List of Individuals:

Sl. No.	Name	Location	Mobile No.
1.	N.Durga Raghuram	Guntur	9848313009
2.	Shailesh Shah	Vadodara	7774002129
3.	Saumya P. Garnaik	Delhi	9871399932
4.	Vivek Shukla	Kopargaon	8960606812
5.	Balaiah Santhapuram	Hyderabad	9110764298
6.	Neeraj Jain	Bhopal	9584786738
7.	Dipak D. Dahake	Nagpur	974 55949031
8.	Dr.Ajay Chandak	Dhule	9823033344
9.	K.D.Bairagi	Ujjain	9907270259
10.	B.Sathyanarayana	Hyderabad	9848810120
11.	Mahesh Kotian	Shimoga	7353590989
12.	Subhash Garg	Hisar	9896095016
13.	Paritosh Awasthi	Bhopal	9300277214
14.	Surathu Ramesh	Vizag	8978081330
15.	P.A.Johny	Thrissur	9400560557
16.	T. Srinivas	Vizag	9490491211
17.	Sreepada Gopikrishna	Vizag	7893006787

CONTENTS

ACKNOWLEDGEMENTS

Publication of the Volume-2 of Vision Document on Mission Sustainable India could be made possible again with the active support of the Team Mission Sustainable India.

I'd like to express my deepest thanks to Shri Arvind Rastogi and Shri Dhananjay S.Kulkarni for helping me with the final checking and fine tuning of the manuscript.

I would like to pay my special regards to Shri R.Vaidyanathan, Accredited Energy Auditor who is my friend and well-wisher since 2006 for writing the Foreword.

This publication would not have been possible without the generous contribution of funds by Mr N.Durga Raghuram from Guntur. I would also like to thank M/s Technovations and Indian Association of Energy Management Professionals for supporting the publication with their advertisements.

Last but not the least, I would like to extend my deepest gratitude to the volunteers of Mission Sustainable India for their continuous support.

(Sunil Kumar Sood)

National Convener, Mission Sustainable India

FOREWORD

I am glad to write the Foreword for the Voulme-2 of Vision Document on Mission Sustainable India. The mission is being coordinated by Shri Sunil Sood, who has been my friend since 2006. He is basically an activist and takes every activity very seriously and undauntedly. This Vision Document was not coming out easily. As all Activists are subjected to problems, so was it with Sunil Sood and his team. The Project was shelved for a few months. An aphorism in Sanskrit says निसर्गः स हि धीराणां यदापद्यधिकं दृढाः It is the nature of brave men to remain even more steadfast in adversity. Sunil Sood stood his ground with even greater determination at those times of difficulties and finally the book has taken shape.

दश कूप समा वापी, दशवापी समोह्रद्रः दशह्रद समः पुत्रो, दश पुत्रोसमो द्रगुः

One step is equal to ten wells. One pond is equal ten step wells, one son is equal to ten ponds and one tree is equal to ten sons. In this way the importance of trees is stressed in the Vedas. This is the importance given to one tree. Our flora and fauna are all equally important. So are all the mineral resources. Petrol has been the cause of some wars. With depleting natural resources, other minerals also will provoke wars, either internal or external.

The book unfolds a Roadmap for take India to a sustainable development path starting from 15th August, 2022. Sustainability is a wide subject and the whole Earth is covered under this. Sustainability cannot be taken just on one area. For example if someone wishes to care for the fauna he may be protecting the wild life in the forest areas. But his doing well for the wildlife may be causing harm to the Forest dwellers who live basically on the forest produce.

De-growth is a must to curtail the over usage of earth's natural wealth. While the industry is restricted to slow down its consumption of Natural Resources we may on the other hand depriving the workers who are solely dependent on the income from the work at the industry. Always the poor are at the receiving end. The influential and rich can get their way at any cost and will not be affected to that extent. So we have to approach Sustainability in a holistic manner. This mission is a compilation and inter-connection of all domains on sustainability and aims at such multi-pronged approach.

In earlier days, Air water and Sunlight were thought to be available in abundance. We can see water has become a commercial item with water bottles on sale all over the world. Tall skyscrapers deprive the neighbours of sunlight. This could become a major issue in the coming days. Air pollution is prevalent and bottled fresh air could be a commercial commodity in the near future. So sustainability is necessary so that our grandchildren and future generations can live safely on this earth.

R Vaidyanathan

Accredited Energy Auditor

PREFACE

The Volume-1 of the Vision Document on Mission Sustainable India covered topics of Sustainable Citizenship, Governance, Bureaucracy, and Justice System.

In the Volume -2, we take some more topics which need to be aligned with Sustainability.

Mission Sustainable India is a people's initiative and people's participation is prominent requirement of this mission to succeed. Hence, a separate chapter on mass communication to educate and create awareness amongst public has been incorporated. Various techniques such as public discourse, use of traditional media, social media, storytelling and framing, affirmation of best practices and examples etc. has been conceived to educate and create awareness among citizens on principles of sustainability based on 5Ps.

Sustainable Education chapter is very close to us and we have tried to do justice to the generations to come. The chapter gives an emphasis on balanced learning based on 5ps with learning by doing and development in an environment conducive to learning process. It provides a holistic development platform to student in diversity of subjects. Here home schooling in primary days of students is given importance with practical learning enhancing cognitive thinking, critical problem solving, and creative thinking. The chapter also gives special importance to informal learning/ Alternative Learning.

Sustainable habitat chapter is a manifestation of problem of slum in metropolitan cities, unsustainable waste management practices, pollution. The chapter suggests solution to such problems such as principle of intelligent Urbanism, balanced development in harmony with nature, balance with nature, technological solution which is part of all other chapters as well, efficiency, conviviality, regional integration, opportunity matrix at el.

Sustainable food and Sustainable Health system chapters are very much integrated. Sustainable health chapter highlights preventive measures to avoid diseases, incentivising healthy life style, promotion of natural health care system. The chapter illustrates what is balanced life style, how to prevent life style. Various measure have been described like minimizing and adequately managing waste and hazardous chemicals, promoting an efficient management of resources, promoting sustainable procurement, reducing health systems' emissions of greenhouse gases and air pollution, prioritizing disease prevention, health promotion and public health services at el.

Sustainable Food System focuses food security measures based on food and vegetables, food without hazardous pesticides and chemicals, non-essentials antibiotics and zero food wastes. In this chapter identification and solution has been suggested for food sustainability. It also explains ways to make sustainable food choices. It suggests locally controlled circular systems that re-integrate and re-localise food and energy production with water and waste management.

We look forward to active support from every one.

7

SUSTAINABLE MASS MEDIA COMMUNICATION

Highlights:

- How can communication processes and information systems contribute to sustainable markets and alternative economic spaces?
- Building Sustainability Agendas—Story Telling, Framing
- Developing strategies for communicating the concept of sustainable development.
- Preventing Negative impacts of mass media

Communication is a process through which we send and receive information. It is derived from the Latin word 'communis' which means 'common'. Communication is a process which increases commonality, but also requires elements of commonality for it to occur at all. In modern society, mass communication is entrusted with the great task of communicating with people from different regions and from varied backgrounds. Communication between a medium and its large audience is called as mass communication. There are multiple ways by which communication is made, and these are collectively known as the "media". The word "media" is plural form of the Latin word 'medium', and it is used as a collective noun to refer to newspapers, magazines, television, radio, films, the internet, Social Networking and blogging sites, etc.

7.1 Sustainable Development and Communication

Sustainable Development has emerged as one of the most prominent development paradigms in the last twenty years. Awareness of the sustainability agenda has also increased as mounting evidence highlights the environmental and social costs of industrial production and mass consumption. However, sustainability presupposes a balance between peoples' present and future needs, and economic, social and environmental capacity to meet those needs, which sits in awkward tension with today's neo-liberal context - faced with financial crisis with scarcity of food and availability of energy.

As interdependencies of communities are growing and local realities are shaped by wider global systems, communication plays a fundamental role in improving knowledge sharing, and encouraging the participation of grassroots and marginalised communities in decisions that shape our future.

In view of the newer global situations, we want to look at communication through new lenses, because mere event based communication would often do more harm than good. We need to have a broader and responsible communication to achieve SD.

Let's take an example, in year 2019 some part of Kolhapur and Pune was deluded with heavy rainfall. Flood was at extreme and such condition was never seen from many decades. When we mean broader and responsible communication- it should take into account what are the prevailing conditions that caused it. Mere high energy, sensational news item for couple of weeks or blaming climate change for it, would be counter-productive.

Though blaming Climate change seems easy option, but it not part of solution. Communication should be to study and instigate the main reasons such as illegal occupation at river banks, illegal mining, etc.

We are proposing this because mere event based communication is often Data driven and at most carefully prepared is Information based.

In Pursuit of sensational news and race of TRP, it of often degraded at the lowest echelon of communication pyramid, i.e. only data driven. This can be most times misleading and counter-productive for the proper communication.

This Vision document wants to have some serious thought on these issues when we consider Mass media Communication for Sustainable Development.

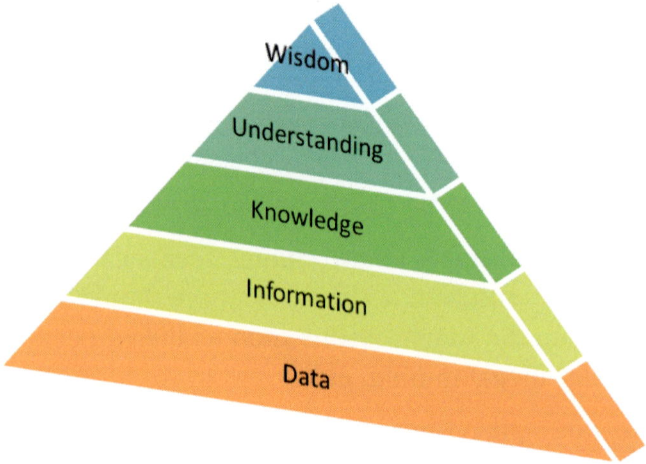

Various forms and levels of Content

Proper communication should be beyond the influence of powerful people and business houses. Biased information is never beneficial for society as a whole.

Key Questions

- How can communication processes and information systems contribute to sustainable markets and alternative economic spaces?
- How can communication processes facilitate the participation of marginalised communities in the global market?
- How can grassroots communities and individuals resist the hegemony of powerful market actors?
- Do mediated discourses undermine or promote ethical and sustainable behaviors?
- How can we promote sustainable behaviors?

The dual pressures of climate change and population growth make enhancing sustainable development an important focus of initiatives hoping to reach as many people as possible with appropriate innovations. Resource and infrastructure challenges often limit the ability of programs to expand through the use of extension and other forms of in-person training. Although media such as radio, television, and mobile phones cannot replace the value of interpersonal communication, they can offer a low-cost alternative for reaching large audiences in even some of the most remote regions. With the increasing use of media for sustainable development questions are raised related to the ability of these channels to move beyond a one-way flow of information to include and respond to local knowledge and experiences and to create dialogue.

7.2 Building Sustainability Agendas—Story Telling, Framing

In general, the general public does not seem to care too much about sustainability—one reason maybe the extreme complexity of SD and vagueness of the concept, which makes it incomprehensible to the target audience. This lack of clarity is far away from the imperative of today's news—dramatic,exciting and sensational. People are becoming more concerned with sustainability issues such as long-term income (prosperity), air and water quality and biodiversity (environment), health (social aspects) or honesty of politicians (democracy). However, most people do not fully appreciate the links between topics, necessary trade-offs, potential risks, and impacts of their behavior. Yet, the sustainability discourse remains fragmented, with a diverse set of challenges receiving vastly different levels of attention.

If sustainable development is too elusive and complex a concept, while particular themes—although catchy and comprehensible—do not provide the bigger picture, then a special strategy for sustainability communication must be employed. However, nothing radically new needed—communication theory points to a role of narratives and explains how media institutions appropriate story-telling when communicating information and news.

In a nutshell: humans use narratives to weave together fragmented observations to construct meanings and realities. For mass media, translating various issues into meaningful stories involves many qualified decisions on how to portray issues in the most vivid and affecting manner possible.

Media theory suggests that developing an interesting narrative or even framing isolated pieces of information through a sustainability concept, and its presentation in media—either textually or visually—could significantly impact how audiences process the information.The mechanism behind media framing is known as applicability effect: i.e., a message has a significantly stronger effect if it resonates with (or is applicable to) the audience's underlying cognitive schemas than if it does not. Experiments prove the effects and importance of the strategic message framing for improving the effectiveness of mediated communication of even neglected sustainability topics.

There have been various conceptual frameworks for sustainability reporting based on themes (e.g., transportation, health), political actions (e.g., SDGs), causality phenomenon (Driving force–Pressure–State–Impact–Response; DPSIR), accounting principle (water or ecosystem accounts), etc. Through a clearly structured organization of relevant information often in the form of indicators, such frameworks enable concise communication and help expose how theinformation provided is related to various processes and how specific policy or management actions can address sustainability problems.

Applying frameworks to analyze and structure information helps to move from data to information and subsequently to the structured knowledge needed to elucidate sustainability issues and to design effective responses.

7.3 Developing strategies for communicating the concept of sustainable development.

Communicating the concept and policy of sustainable development is very challenging and specific. This is a result of its complexity, abstractness and wide conceptual scope, the large number of key participants, the wide spectrum of target audiences and partners, not forgetting the existence of differing perception of the concept itself and the very policy of sustainable development. Some of the specific approaches which can be considered are discussed in the following paragraphs.

7.3.1 A positive approach, the opening up of better perspectives for life, and not being intimidated by the worst-case scenario

At first sight, the easiest way to explain the necessity of implementing the SD concept is to show the consequences of breaching the rules of sustainable development. Regardless of how opportune it might seem, this kind of approach could result in developing strong negative feelings towards the idea itself as well as creating animosities, which could hamper the creation of any consensus on the need to respect the norms of SD. Some scientific explanations, which aim to alert the public to the imperative of sustainable development, frequently use catastrophic scenarios of future life on the Earth, showing what would ensue if there were no significant changes made.

Instead of intimidating with the worst-case scenario, the Mission SI-22 suggests a distinctly positive approach, which places its emphasis on the opening up of new developmental opportunities and perspectives. By stirring up such positive (and not negative) emotions, the concept could obtain the necessary wide ranging support and initiate the necessary level of public activism at all levels.

7.3.2 Speaking with the same voice, translating the SD concept into the language of utter clarity

Communicating the SD concept is a very challenging task, foremost because of its abstractness and complexity. Hence, it is necessary to invest special effort to translate this idea into the language of utter clarity, which will not confuse, but encourage and mobilize for concrete action. In addition to using the basic messages from this Communication strategy, it is recommended to highlight concrete positive examples, promote good local experiences as well as to encourage the creation of informal action slogans by different actors in the process.

7.3.3 Encouraging public dialogue

It is hard to stress enough how important the developing of a wide ranging public dialogue about SD is for the effective communication of this development concept. Only in this way, will it be possible to mobilize, encourage and ensure a wide level of participation, and, consequently, create the space needed to transform positive feelings into a change in behavior by the widest possible circle of public actors and citizens. Within this context, an honest and not propaganda-style approach is being recommended, as a consistent application of the concept and the idea of SD implies the taking of responsibility for some difficult decisions with a long-term significance. The public dialogue should be advocated through all channels, ranging from the traditional media to the web sphere and direct contacts. Organizing public events such as round tables, panel discussions, public lectures, are traditionally good communication dialogue channels.

7.3.4 Emphasis at the local level

Every abstract concept is best explained by its reduction to specific life issues that are visible daily to everyone. These, by rule, occur at the local level, and as a result, this is where the emphasis should be in the communication approach. Any full scale national events and campaigns, analyses, and declarative commitment will remain isolated and abstract unless accompanied by concrete local activities. Hence, the local self-governance level should be given a special role in the implementation of this Strategy.

7.3.5 The role of the traditional mass media

The Vision Document sees the media not only as an important target group, but as primary partners in the implementation of the communication strategy. The mass media shall, naturally, serve not only as the main channel for initiating and developing a wide ranging public debate on the concept of sustainable development, but also play an active role in it, which rightly belongs to them.

During this debate, various disagreements and dissonant tones may realistically be expected, which would be normal and to be expected even in societies with a lower degree of tendencies towards political conflicts than ours. Although there is nothing wrong in such public weighing of arguments pro et contra, there is a certain degree of risk that such "tough" discussions may set an undesirable tone to the whole communication process.

Therefore, it is recommended that the mass media (particularly private television channels), besides regular reporting activities, create special program contents, which would represent the SD concept in both, an amusing and attractive way.

It is also recommended that Public Broadcasting Services like Doordarshan, AIR classify support for the concept of sustainable development as one of its primary program commitments. Such a possibility is also open with the private media, which may be treated as part of their contribution to the concept of socially responsible business activities. In both cases, it would mean the creation of space for free marketing programming of public advocacy, which would significantly reduce costs and increase the "cost to benefit ratio" of the whole process.

7.3.6 The Social Media

If the traditional media (press, radio and TV) is as a rule aimed at the lower and middle class and use emotions as the most efficient way to form public opinion, then their role has to be enriched with the contents of the social media related to the web sphere – podcasts, blogs, portals, face book... and other types of online communication. This channel is suitable not only for the coming generations, but also for that part of the population with higher education experience and expert knowledge, who gives priority to rational argumentation and concrete facts when forming their attitudes.

Newer ways to sensitize public opinion should be used, either by Podcasts, YouTube, or gaming platforms. There is huge potential emerging in these newer ways of communications that can be tapped.

7.3.7 Affirmation of best practice and examples

The affirmation of best practice and examples of the application of the SD concept is an irreplaceable tool, which will enliven the concept and provide it with concrete types and forms of appearance. Therefore, the practice of introducing regular awards for the best examples from the practice in the areas of basic pillars of sustainable development is recommended, including culture and ethics as well.

Since there is no good communication without a creative approach, annual awards for the best communicating of the concept of sustainable development are also recommended. Thereby the existing creative communication potential of society would be motivated. For example, TV games/ contests like "Kaun Banega Crorepati" can be developed for promotion of SD. An attempt was made by a group of persons who conceived a scheme "Kaun Banega Conservepati" (to link the game with conservation and sustainability)

7.3.8 Emphasized responsibility of the business sector and promotion of the concept of corporate social responsibility

The promotion of socially responsible corporate practice in the business sector is a strong mechanism in the promotion of the concept of sustainable development. Giving emphasis to examples of business activities valuing the trinity "People, Planet, Profit" has far-reaching and multiple social effects. The practice of regular awards for best examples of sustainable business activities and the implementation of the corporate social responsibility principles it is highly recommendable here as well.

7.3.9 Mobilizing the "ambassador" of sustainable development -personalization of the concept

The employment of popular personalities from different generations and profiles, enjoying popularity and respect from the different target groups, who are at the same time genuine devotees to sustainable development, is one of the most secure roads to the hearts of most citizens. These carefully selected "ambassadors" of sustainable development and their active involvement in the process may multiply the results of communication activities.

Newer ways for ambassadors, means not only it as being the most influential or famous person, but really impacting and near to the society can be made. We need to find out the ways for it.

One way can be- a rolling ambassador student per class to sensitize the issues related to Sustainability. One Child among them is studying and telling others about it, wouldn't it be an ideal learning process and social change. In backdrop of New Education Policy-2020, we hope to see such changes emerging from the school. This is not limited to schools only and can be extended to other institutions and sectors. We can definitely look for such opportunities.

7.3.10 Economically and politically powerful individuals as pioneers of the concept (nationally and locally)

The reality is that such sweeping changes require the involvement of people with political and economic power in society in communicating SD. Since one of the objectives of this document is to encourage the taking of social responsibility for success in the implementation of the Strategy of Sustainable Development, it is not objectively achievable without the active involvement of the supporters of the concept from the political and business areas. Different political and business organizations have to select such "pioneers" very carefully, constantly keeping in mind the imperative of building the widest possible social consensus.

7.3.11 Avoid the trap of identifying the concept of sustainable development with green issues

The use of the existing positive feelings related to "green issues" may serve only as a starting position, because one of the key communication tasks is to ensure the understanding of sustainable development as being a considerably broader and more complex issue than simply environmental protection.

7.3.12 Activating the consciousness of consumers

One of the global trends in promoting sustainable development is the introduction of certifications, labels, and certificate on product compliance with SD for a multitude of products, which are consumed every day. In this way, growing awareness of consumers may be used as one of the mechanisms, which help the concept of sustainable development spread and benefit market at the same time. Therefore, it is recommended to take over such aspects from the business sector, consumers' associations, and relevant non-governmental organizations.

7.3.13 Activate "new ideas" by raising the public, children's and young people's awareness of SD

Raising this sectors awareness of the concept itself, the role of which has both, an educational and novel character – by helping them to view development in a new, balanced way – represents an integral, and maybe even the most significant part in promoting and articulating the concept of sustainable development.

In cooperation with educational institutions at all levels (higher education, secondary and primary schools) it is necessary to explain and promote these new ideas and the spirit of exploration of this target group through the organization of quizzes, competitions and the publishing of papers and ideas. This would stress the importance of every individual, especially the younger generations, in the developing and implementation of the sustainable development concept, which would, consequently, strengthen the depth of communication and spread the idea to the widest circles of the community.

Final Note

Communication for SD is nothing but the concise and accurate communication of the impending dangers of unsustainable pattern of consumption and economy. Many times this data comes from the Research Institutions and therefore may not be palatable to common people, therefore media powered to act in this specific issues, should try to make it understandable by most of the people and try to form a well-understood public opinion.

8

SUSTAINABLE EDUCATION

Highlights:

- Child and Family specific Home-Schooling/Self-Learning/ Natural learning with Online support.
- Curriculum should be based on 5 Ps and Pedagogy based on "Whole Universe is our Class Room"
- Promotion of Neighbourhood Facilitation and Activities Centres
- Existing private schools can also be utilized as community schools/ vocational training centres.
- Existing Government schools can also be utilized as Hands-on/practical/ experiential learning and activities centres or play grounds.

As we are all aware, our education system, specially the primary and secondary education system has not been able to keep pace with the times. The system is not having any space for the needs of the special children as well as those who would like to pursue their passion and lead their life as they wish to. There is about 45 % drop-out rate from 1st to 10th standard for various reasons. One of the key reasons revealed by the drop outs is that they do not find schools interesting and useful. Only 25% of the students who pass out in 12th standard join colleges.

Good news is - the National Education Policy (NEP) -2020 has been approved by the government recently. It is expected to bring the necessary changes required. The NEP is the outcome of a mammoth exercise and a firm commitment from the top leadership for drafting an education policy that will change the outlook towards students and consider everyone in the system as a knowledge-seeker.

The policy attempts a significant overhaul of the education system - right from terminologies and institutional frameworks to functionality - when it comes to transforming governance, delivery and financing of education.

It is heartening to note that the NEP talks of aligning education with the Sustainable Development Goal-4 (Quality Education).The Mission suggests a Curriculum based on 5Ps and Pedagogy based on "Whole Universe Is Our Class Room" to align sustainability with education. These suggestions can be considered for drafting of National Curriculum Framework to be prepared as per the NEP.

8.1 History of British Education System in India

8.1.1 English Education Act 1835 - The beginning of the end of Indian Traditional Education System

The English Education Act 1835 was a legislative Act of the Council of India, gave effect to a decision in 1835 by Lord William Bentinck, then Governor-General of British India, to reallocate funds the East India Company was required by the British Parliament to spend on education and literature in India. They had not supported tradition of Muslim and

Hindu education and the publication of literature in the native learned tongues (Sanskrit and Persian); henceforward they were to support establishments teaching a Western curriculum with English as the language of instruction. Together with other measures promoting English as the language of administration and of the higher law courts (replacing Persian), this led eventually to English becoming one of the languages of India, rather than simply the native tongue of its foreign rulers.

In discussions leading up to the Act Thomas Babington Macaulay **produced his famous Memorandum on (Indian) Education which was scathing on the inferiority (as he saw it) of native (particularly Hindu) culture and learning. He argued that Western learning was superior, and currently could only be taught through the medium of English. There was therefore a need to produce—by English-language higher education**—"a class of persons, Indian in blood and colour, but English in taste, in opinions, in morals and in intellect" who could in their turn develop the tools to transmit Western learning in the vernacular languages of India.

Among Macaulay's recommendations were the immediate stopping of the printing by the East India Company of Arabic and Sanskrit books and that the Company should not continue to support traditional education beyond "the Sanskrit College at Benares and the Mahometan College at Delhi" (which he considered adequate to maintain traditional learning).

The Act itself, however, took a less negative attitude to traditional education and was soon succeeded by further measures based upon the provision of adequate funding for both approaches. Vernacular language education, however, continued to receive little funding, although it had not been much supported before 1835 in any case.

Macaulay's "Minute Upon Indian Education"

To remove all doubt, however, Macaulay produced and circulated a Minute on the subject. Macaulay argued that support for the publication of books in Sanskrit and Arabic should be withdrawn, support for traditional education should be reduced to funding for the Madrassa at Delhi **and the Hindu College at** Benares, but students should no longer be paid to study at these establishments. The money released by these steps should instead go to fund education in Western subjects, with English as the language of instruction. He summarised his argument:

> *To sum up what I have said, I think it is clear that we are not fettered by the Act of Parliament of 1813; that we are not fettered by any pledge expressed or implied; that we are free to employ our funds as we choose; that we ought to employ them in teaching what is best worth knowing; that English is better worth knowing than Sanskrit or Arabic; that the natives are desirous to be taught English, and are not desirous to be taught Sanskrit or Arabic; that neither as the languages of law, nor as the languages of religion, have the Sanskrit and Arabic any peculiar claim to our engagement; that it is possible to make natives of this country thoroughly good English scholars, and that to this end our efforts ought to be directed.*

Macaulay's comparison of Arabic and Sanskrit literature to what was available in English is forceful, colourful, and nowadays often quoted against him.

> *I have conversed both here and at home with men distinguished by their proficiency in the Eastern tongues..... I have never found*

one among them who could deny that a single shelf of a good European library was worth the whole native literature of India and Arabia.Honours might be roughly even in works of the imagination, such as poetry, but when we pass from works of imagination to works in which facts are recorded, and general principles investigated, the superiority of the Europeans becomes absolutely immeasurable."

8.1.2 Development of Education Policies and Curriculum Framework

Until 1976, Indian constitution allowed the state governments to take decisions on all matters pertaining to school education including curriculum. The centre could only provide guidance to the states on policy issues. It was under such circumstances that the initial attempts of National Education Policy of 1968 and the Curriculum Framework designed by National Council of Educational Research and Training (NCERT) in 1975 were formulated.

NCERT developed NCF in 1975 following the recommendations of Education Policy on 1968. In 1976, the constitution was amended to include education in the concurrent list, and for the first time in 1986 the country as a whole had a National Policy on Education (NPE-1986) which envisions National Curriculum Framework as a means of modernising education. The Policy proposed a national framework of curriculum as a means of evolving a national system of education capable of responding to India's geographical and cultural diversity while ensuring a common core values and a comparable standards of education. NPE-1986 emphasised a relevant, flexible and learner-centred curriculum.

It recommended a common core component in school education throughout the country. The policy also entrusted the NCERT with the responsibility of developing the National Curriculum Framework and reviewing the framework at frequent intervals. Hence, in 1988 NCERT prepared the National Curriculum Framework for school education based on the recommendations of NPE-1986. After that it was felt that curriculum needs to be flexible and relevant to meet the needs of diverse learners. Also issues of curriculum load and examinations stress needed attention. Therefore, National Curriculum Framework was reviewed in the year 2000 and then in 2005 and the latest NCF-2005 appeared as a result of this review.

- NCF-1975 Following recommendation of Education Policy in 1968
- NCF-1988 Following recommendation of Education Policy in 1986
- NCF-2000 Revised NCF-1988
- NCF-2005 Revised NCF-2000

In India, NCERT develops National Curriculum Framework which provides guidelines for developing syllabi and textbooks and school curriculum. NCF-2005 prepared by NCERT discusses a wide range of issues concerning school education. The framework discusses aims of education; epistemological assumption about nature and forms of knowledge; and assumptions about learner and learning. It places learner at the centre and gives primacy to voices and experiences of learners. The framework views that knowledge is evolving in nature and is created involving learners as active participants in the process of knowledge construction.

NCF-2005 recommends curricular areas to be taught at different stages of school education. The NCF-2005 also recommends that Arts education and Physical and Health education should be made curricular subjects at elementary and secondary stage and optional subjects at higher secondary stage. It also discusses the objectives and pedagogy of these subjects. It recommends that assessment of learner should be made an integral part of school life. It also discusses the necessary systemic reforms including examination reforms and teacher education reforms to achieve the aims of education. Some discussion about enabling school environment is also given in NCF-2005. NCF-2005 reiterates the recommendations of National Policy on Education (NPE-1986).

The National Curriculum Framework provides the basic structure for the teaching practices implemented in the educational programme of schools in our country. The syllabus and curriculum followed by the schools is based on the NCF. After the review process begins, focus groups will be formed to look into the scrutinizing of proposals for school education in our country. The new NCF is expected to be finalized by the year 2021.

8.1.3 Aims of Education*

**Excerpts from the report by Focus Group on the Aims of Education constituted by the National Council of Educational Research and Training (NCERT)*

For a fairly long time now, we have been engaged in the great task of educating the children of India, an independent nation with a rich variegated history, extraordinarily complex cultural diversity, and commitment to democratic values and general well-being. Given the enormity and importance of this task, it is necessary that we create occasions from time to time to sit back collectively and ask ourselves, 'What are we doing in our engagement with this task? Is there a need to ask ourselves afresh some of the basic questions such as what ought to be the purpose of education?'

If we look at what the school education system has done in the last decades, perhaps we have much to be satisfied with. Products of this system have gone on to make their mark in diverse fields of national and international life. But there is also a deep disquiet about several aspects of our educational system, particularly the school system. The disquiet springs from a variety of factors, such as:

(a) the school system has come to be characterized with a kind of inflexibility that makes it very difficult to breathe fresh life into it;

(b) learning for children seems to have become a sort of isolated and perfunctory activity which they are unable to connect in any organic or vital way with the rest of their life;

(c) education has come to be perceived more and more as a means of ensuring the future 'well-being' of students (i.e., their place in society and their economic status which guarantees this place)—this has led to a neglect of children's present abilities and difficulties, which could deprive them of a quality of life much richer in content than that the education system prepares them for;

(d) what is presented and transmitted as knowledge in schools leaves out vital constituents of man's epistemic enterprise; and

(e) schools promote a regime of thought which discourages thinking and precludes new and surprising insights.

There are, however, issues relating to education about which we have a fairly clear idea and about which there ought to be general agreement to a large extent. It would be helpful to seek an answer to the question 'what ought to be the aims of education?' by way of our engagement with these issues:

(i) School education is a deliberate and more-or less external intervention in the life of a child. Although much learning and teaching takes place at home, in the neighbourhood community, and in actual living communities in rural and tribal India, the school introduces the child to an environment of teaching and learning that, quite by design, marks itself off from the rest of the child's environment. Tagore's experience of his first day at school is repeated with greater or less intensity in most children's first encounter with school: "...all of a sudden I found my world vanishing from around me, giving place to wooden benches and straight walls staring at me with the blank stare of the blind." While the school must perhaps have boundaries of its own—as the life of the school cannot just be merged with the life of the community around it—these boundaries must not become barriers. They must, on the other hand, facilitate the creation of vital links between children's experiences at home and in the community and what the school offers them.

(ii) Self-knowledge is diametrically opposed to self-ignorance and self-deception. To be deceived by others is bad but to be deceived by oneself is even worse. However, unfortunately, we deceive ourselves much of the time. The big fat ego, which most of us have, can remain fat only on a daily diet of self-deception. Self-knowledge can be achieved only through the knowledge of the other, and one cannot know the other without being just to the other. Education must be a continuous process of self-discovery, of learning the truth about oneself. This is a lifelong process; but the school, through insightful teaching and learning situations of various kinds, can bring home to the child the great importance of this process.

(iii) There is need to convince the child or the adolescent of the superiority of a life of virtues to a life of vice and wickedness. The only way to do this is to effectively demonstrate that genuine human happiness can spring only from a life lived in accordance with virtues. But, how is this to be done? How is one to counter the opposite belief that it is not the virtues but power and wealth that are constitutive of true happiness? In a world where the latter belief is pre-dominant, it may be impossible to teach the value of virtues to our children. We need, therefore, to create the possibility of profound questioning of our social structure, and show in various ways the deep connection between human discontent and a life devoid of virtues.

(iv) Cultural diversity is one of our greatest gifts. To respect and do justice to others is also to respect and do justice to their respective cultures or communities. We, therefore, need to radically change the centre versus periphery perspective on intercultural relationships in our country. Cultures on the so-called periphery must receive as much attention as cultures in the centre. As for education, its implication is that ways of life other than one's own must be imaginatively and effectively presented as deserving of as much respect as one's own.

(v) Individual differences are as important as cultural differences. Individual children frequently have capacities and skills which do not find adequate recognition in the school environment. Development and flourishing of these skills and capacities would not only enhance the individual's life but also enrich the life of the community. Education must therefore promote and nourish as wide a range of capacities and skills in our children as possible. The gamut of such skills include the performing arts (music, dance, drama,, and so on), painting and crafts, and literary abilities (weaving stories, wielding language to portray different aspects of life, a flair for metaphorical and poetic expression, etc.). Also, skills as diverse as some children's special capacity to bond with nature—with trees, birds, and animals—need to be nurtured.

(vi) Knowledge is not a unitary concept. There are different kinds of knowledge as well as different ways of knowing. The idea that objectivity, which is a necessary constituent of knowledge, can be achieved only if knowledge is free from emotions (care, concern, and love) must be abandoned. One implication of this for education is that literary and artistic creativity is as much part man's epistemic enterprise as is seeking knowledge through laboratory experiments or deductive reasoning. The former frequently enables us to see the truth in a way that the paradigmatic scientific quest cannot.

(vii) Education must be seen as a liberating process; otherwise, all that has been said so far will be rendered pointless. The process of education must therefore free itself from the shackles of all kinds of exploitation and injustice (e.g., poverty, gender discrimination, caste and communal bias), which prevent our children from being part of the process.

(viii) It is very important that school teaching and learning takes place in an environment that is aesthetically pleasing. It is also essential that children take an active part in creating such an environment for themselves.

(ix) It ought to be possible for every child to be proud of his or her nation. But, one can be proud of something only if it is an achievement of one's own or if one is very intimately connected with those whose achievement it is. We can be proud of our own achievements, or the achievements of our children or friends. If we feel an intimacy with God or nature, we can be proud of even the skies and the whole universe. It is therefore very important that education fosters within the child an intimacy with people who are directly connected with achievements which are part of our national heritage. It is of course equally important to see that children's pride in their own nation does not negate their pride in the great achievements of humanity as a whole.

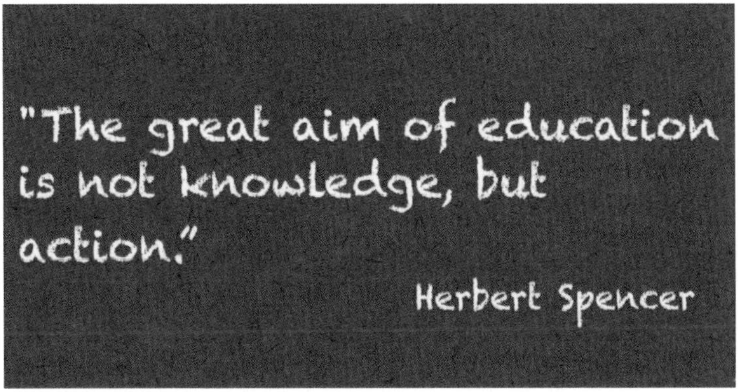

8.2 Home-Schooling/ Self-Learning

Self-Learning/Home-schooling are the terms used to include education choices where a child does not go to a formal school. While most of the time this means that parents assume responsibility for the child's education in a home environment, it can also mean parents who travel a lot with children as a source of learning, or special tutors engaged to teach specific subjects or even parent cooperatives and intentional communities that collectively educate a group of children.

The parent has the option to tcach thc child more effectively in the best possible school which can be done by resorting to home-schooling method as well. It is submitted that there is no absolute bar in the Right ToEducation Act preventing a parent from ensuring that his child is educated through self-learning/home-schooling method.

The option of Home-Schooling/Self-Learning is considered for at least one of the following reasons:

(i) **Religious** – Some parents feel that the value system of their family is undermined by schools, or that they need to include more of their belief systems in their children's everyday education. This has traditionally been one of the larger groups of homeschoolers.

(ii) **Philosophical** – Some parents believe that today's educational institutions inhibit true learning and growth. Included in this group might be parents who believe that older methods of education are more effective, as well as parents who feel that they should take advantage of advances in technology to provide a better education for their children.

(iii) **Problem-Solving** – This group is the least evident in most homeschooling books or websites, but it might actually represent the single largest group. These parents had their children in school at one point, but they were disappointed by the experience. In trying to solve problems and do what's best for their children, they have selected homeschooling as the best option.

This third group often starts homeschooling with the least amount of preparation. In many cases, the decision to homeschool is triggered by some incidents that bring to a climax years of frustration with traditional schools. They turn to homeschooling only because they feel that the system that they had relied on has let them down; that they are homeschooling more as an accident than out of conviction. Some feel that since they are homeschooling only to help out their child, this sets them apart from other homeschoolers.

Of course, these three groups do not encompass every family that chooses to homeschool. There is an idea among homeschoolers that there might be as many reasons to homeschool as there are families that take advantage of home education. Your reasons to homeschool might be one of the above reasons, a combination of these reasons, or something entirely different.

What is Self-Learning/ Home-Schooling?

- It is the education of children at their homes rather than at a school.
- It is about providing a learning environment to the children in their homes to shape their horizons and customize their learning beyond confines of the formal schooling system.
- It is about self-learning with support from Parents/ Mentors
- It is about parents understanding what their children like
- It is about happiness of the Children
- It is about problem solving and not rote learning
- It is about creativity and not conformity
- It is about understanding that teachers are not required for learning
- **It is not about tuitions at home by tutors**

8.2.1 Why Self-Learning/Home Schooling?

- The Home-schooling concept is being increasingly accepted as a better alternative to the conventional education for the various advantages it offers:
- Schools fundamentally disconnect us from nature, physical work, families, communities, local languages, our wisdom and real-world issues,
- High homework pressure, heavy bags, and punishments.
- When parents provide their kid with the home-schooling option, a stronger connection is built between the child and the parent.
- Students learn at the pace that suits them and focus on subjects that interest them more. The hours are also tweaked to suit both parents and students.
- Parents devise their own ways of teaching children at home, and the hours for teaching vary from parent to parent.

8.2.2 The benefits of Self-Learning/home-schooling

The parents have control over what their children learn.

- Helps build good relationships and bond with the children.
- Provides flexibility over teaching timings.
- Provides an opportunity to make learning exciting through your innovative learning ideas
- Helps provide necessary attention to your kids.

- Provides an opportunity that aids in practical learning experiences
- Protects your wards from the negativity of the society.
- Provides an opportunity to pass on your values and beliefs to your children.
- An opportunity to provide attention to subjects where your kid lacks attention.
- Helps in conveying your self-earned tricks and shortcuts for easy and fast learning.
- Helps in teaching your kids in a better and an effective manner by developing a one-to-one relationship with them.
- An opportunity for your kids to learn great lessons from your life experiences
- Helps make your kids believe that education can be exciting and fun
- Helps in making parents aware of their children's hidden talents
- It also helps initiate discussion between parents and kids where the parents can also learn from children

8.2.3 Concerns about Self-Learning/Home-schooling

- It can lead to frustrations in kids as they can't enjoy school and make new friends
- This can sometimes make kids go into depression as they have no or minimal interactions outside their home.

- There will be days when parents will not be able to give entire attention to kids. At that time they may lag behind in studies.
- You will be in constant worry about your kid's education and not be able to relax much even after coming from long hours of work.
- Large costs are involved in home-schooling as the study material, and other resources need to be bought, and parents have to bear all of it on their shoulders.
- Sometimes parents may lack patience when teaching kids. This, in turn, may lead to your kids getting distant from you.
- No overall knowledge of all the subjects.
- No further opportunities as colleges ask for schooling certificates when seeking admissions.
- Irregular learning as parents may have their personal commitments that may prevent them from daily teaching sessions.

The above concerns can be effectively addressed by setting up "Facilitation and Activities Centres" at every locality.

8.3 The need to align education with Sustainability

A group of US researchers estimated the value of the goods and services the natural world provides to the global economy - it was nearly twice the value of what humans were themselves making. So there is a huge amount at stake. UNEP estimates that 40% of the global economy is based on biological products and processes.

The National Education Policy 2020 envisions an India centred education system that contributes directly to transforming our nation sustainably into an equitable and vibrant knowledge society, by providing high quality education to all.

The direction of the global education development agenda is reflected in the sustainable development goal 4 (SDG4) of the 2030 Agenda for Sustainable Development. SDG4 seeks to "ensure inclusive and equitable quality education and promote lifelong learning opportunities for all" by 2030. Five of the seven targets of SDG4 focus on quality education and learning outcomes. SDG4 is, therefore, an all-encompassing goal, which is applicable to every nation attempting to bring quality of life to its citizens in a sustainable way, without degrading the environment. This is a huge challenge and the understanding of this should begin in the early part of education. Another dimension of the future of education is the need to deal with the connected dimensions of education. Knowledge will be transformative because of the manner in which it will be connected to all domains. An overarching aspect of SDG4 is that of inclusion and fostering quality education, and in order to be a practitioner in the field of education, one needs to have some orientation to this mode of thinking.

8.4 Binding Framework for 5 Ps of sustainable development

Schooled or no-schooled, learning has to happen from life for every individual. Given the right conditions and impetus every child from infancy to adulthood is capable of learning by himself with interest and joy. Self-learning is not just the best but the only form of learning. Teachers' role should be no more than a facilitator supervisor and protector.

What makes a child learn by himself with joy and self-motivation?

1. Necessity to do something or solve a problem
2. Out of curiosity to know, and/or find out meaning, and or discover something
3. Find joy of creating or doing

A child needs a supervising parental/adult guidance and supportive infrastructure/ provisions to keep him safe and spirited as he/she takes her stride in learning at his own pace to reach his or her own goal/collective societal goal.

Time to time a learner may need to get assessed of his knowledge achieved in a subject to allow him to be standardised by an external system be it an academic institution or professional experts or social or governmental organisation.

Having said that, learning is not just collecting information on a subject to pass a graded assessment, it is about acquiring ability to do something meaningful, find meaning of something, feel the beauty, purpose, joy in the subject and raise collective peace, well being, prosperity and partnerships of all people and planet ecosystems.

In any natural ecosystem, stability and resilience comes from the diversity of species and level of interconnectedness through predator prey relation or mutualism for survival. An ecosystem is deemed prosperous when all species population thrives interdependently but there is no explosion in population in one species. Whenever there has been explosion of one species, natural forces have been active to balance the equilibrium. The human society which is up to cause its self-destruction through war, violence, fight for natural resources is an example of this existential crisis.

Hence, humankind have got to learn how to lead a balance life on this planet for their own survival. It is already a phenomenon that children with their uncluttered intelligence and soulful bliss are discovering this planet saving wisdom by themselves ahead of the adults as they are the ones to be worst hit by the ravages of climate change caused by the 200 years of industrial civilization.

How the concepts of Sustainable Development should reflect in a child'seducation from infancy to adulthood.

(i) PLANET (Environmental Sustainability): Protect our planet's natural resources and climate for future generations.

Planet focused education for humans as the most evolved species of animals is to protect and guard the flow and sustenance of life and not destroy the unique diversity of life in the biosphere of the planet. Planet centric education requires purposeful education involving all necessary sciences to harmonize and not disrupt the partnerships of all forms of life that have been cohabiting the earth for millions of years without any existential crisis.

(ii) PEOPLE (Social Sustainability): End poverty and hunger in all forms and ensure dignity and equality.

People centric education is education that gives power to the people to feel their own worth irrespective of the segment of society they belong, encouraging them to work towards a class free just society or unbiased opportunity where value of work rests upon service to fellow beings and natural ecosystem and not to the positions of power.

(iii) PROSPERITY (Economic Sustainability): Ensure prosperous and fulfilling lives in harmony with nature.

Prosperity centric education is one that creates food, sustenance, beauty, joy, design efficiency but no net waste. Instead of infinite production, consumption, dehumanization, exploitation of human/animal lives, excess and waste creation for economic profits, education should redefine prosperity to be improvement in transforming, reusing and evolving of human intellect, harmonized cohabitations of diverse communities and manufacturing of commodities that leave zero waste footprint in nature.

(iv) PEACE: Foster peaceful, just and inclusive societies.

Peacekeeping - education is one which treats every individual (plant/ human/ animal) in nature with respect for its true value of existence, not just its apparent commercial value.

It begins at home and grows to the level of community, society, nation and then the planet. It also teaches freedom from fear to fight any force that disrespects this fundamental value of everyone's peace against smaller personal interests. Industry that exploits land for minerals and destroys forest and natural ecosystems is a war against peace.

(v) PARTNERSHIP: Implement the agenda through a solid global partnership.

Partnership in education means education cannot be restricted within the four walls of the class room for some 3-6 hours a day; it can equally happen from any teacher from any walk of life and at any age when that knowledge is most necessary. Thinking global ideas and acting local is the purpose of this type of education.

Partnerships at all levels within a community are the source of its stability.

8.5 Recommendations of MSI-22 for Sustainable Education

Our recommendation is limited to the early child hood to secondary education for the age groups of 3 to 18 years. For higher education, we just wish to say that higher education should be need based and must be pursued with clear goals and not to acquire a degree. The NEP-2020 is a good document for higher education.

8.5.1 Recognition to Non-Formal/ Informal/ Alternative Education

Informal education is a general term for education that can occur outside of a structured curriculum. Informal education encompasses student interests within a curriculum in a regular classroom, but is not limited to that setting. It works through conversation, and the exploration and enlargement of experience.

Non-formal education refers to education that occurs outside the formal school system. Non-formal education is often used interchangeably with terms such as community education, adult education, lifelong education and second-chance education.

Alternate schools are characterized by a non-competitive, multilingual learning environment; a broader curriculum that is more locally adapted; a more continuous and qualitative non – comparative assessment; a pace of learning that is determined bya child's capacity; inclusiveness of all children regardless of disabilities, academic excellence or financial background; and the use of a range of teaching methodologies that are responsive to different children's needs.

- They also act as active educational resource centres. Out of them has emerged theory in the areas of Educational Philosophy, Sociology, Language Studies, as well as a range of teaching-learning methodologies etc.
- They are also very closely associated with the development of changes in educational pedagogy and philosophy in India

8.5.2 Establishing a National Council for Alternative Schooling

- Council could potentially work out a set of criteria and develop an accreditation process.

  To eliminate any misuse of this label by schools that intend to function as 'teaching shops'.
- In addition these centres could be supported by the Council to serve as model schools, contribute to developing materials and better pedagogic methods.

8.5.3 Setting up of Neighbourhood Facilitation and Activities Centres for Home-Schooling/Self-Learning Kids.

The government should recognize support setting up of Neighbour Facilitation and Activities centres to address the concerns of Home-Schooling/Self-Learning kids and parents as mentioned under clause 8.2.2. These centres must be set up at every locality.

More than 5 Lakh such centres are needed as per our estimates. An example of such a centre is "Griha Shiksha Kendra"(GSK) which has been established at Bhopal.

Griha Shiksha Kendra (GSK) is an Innovative Model of Education combining formal, non-formal and informal systems of education with curriculum framework focused on 5 Ps of Sustainability and Pedagogy based on "Whole Universe is our Class Room".

Being a model of 'Sustainable Education', it relies mostly on existing unutlised or under-utilised infrastructure and expertise from retired persons, mentors and volunteers while putting the children on self-learning path.

हर बच्चा स्वयं शिक्षक, हर बच्चा स्वयं सेवक।
हर बच्चा एक खोजी; हर बच्चा मनमौजी।

Such centres can be promoted by a group of parents as well as by the Resident Welfare Associations for their children as well as the children living in the vicinity. It can also help the children of migrant workers and the school drop outs.

The details of the activities carried out in the centre are available in their Facebook page: https://www.facebook.com/SustainableEducationAtHome/

8.5.4 Utilization/ Conversion of existing Private/ Government Schools for Hands-On/Practical trainings, community learning centres/Vocational training centres/ Play grounds/Parks etc

We propose that the existing schools shall be utilised less for theoretical lectures and more for all experiential learning. That will help in integrating formal and non-formal modes of learning and to prepare the children for life skills as well the professional skills.

8.5.5 Strengthening and popularising of NIOS and State Open Boards

The self-learner's needs for certification/examinations are being met presently by the "National Institute of Open Schooling (NIOS) and some Open Boards set up by the state governments. However, these need to be strengthened and made popular so that the parents find the self-learning path easier to follow. The existing infrastructure of the schools may be made available to NIOS and State Open Boards for conduct of mentoring and guidance centres.

9

SUSTAINABLE HABITAT

Highlights:

- De-Growth of existing over-crowded cities and towns
- Promotion of Auroville type self-sustaining community living.
- Limit to growths to be fixed for all small towns
- Integrating Urban and Rural planning for Sustainable Habitat

A '*sustainable*' **habitat** is an ecosystem that produces food and shelter for people and other organisms, without resource depletion and in such a way that no external waste is produced. Thus the habitat can continue into future tie without external infusions of resource. Such a sustainable habitat may evolve naturally or be produced under the influence of man. A sustainable habitat that is created and designed by human intelligence will mimic nature, if it is to be successful. Everything within it is connected to a complex array of organisms, physical resources and functions. Organisms from many different biomes can be brought together to fulfill various *ecological niches*.

The term often refers to sustainable human habitats, which typically involve some form of green building or environmental planning. In creating the sustainable habitats, environmental scientists, designers, engineers and architects must consider no element as a waste product to be disposed of somewhere off site, but as a nutrient stream for another process to feed on. Researching ways to interconnect waste streams to production creates a more sustainable society by minimizing pollution.

The Mission SI-22 considers that sustainable habitat can be best achieved by following the principles of intelligent urbanism. These have been discussed in the following paragraphs.

9.1 Principles of intelligent urbanism

Principles of intelligent urbanism (PIU) is a theory of urban planning composed of a set of ten axioms intended to guide the formulation of city plans and urban designs. They are intended to reconcile and integrate diverse urban planning and management concerns. These axioms include environmental sustainability, heritage conservation, appropriate technology, infrastructure-efficiency, place making, social access, transit-oriented development, regional integration, human scale, and institutional integrity. The term was coined by Prof. Christopher Charles Benninger.

The PIU evolved from the city planning guidelines formulated by the International Congress of Modern Architecture (CIAM), the urban design approaches developed at Harvard's pioneering Urban Design Department under the leadership of Josep Lluis Sert, and the concerns enunciated by Team Ten. It is most prominently seen in plans prepared by Christopher Charles Benninger and his numerous colleagues in the Asian context (Benninger 2001). They form the elements of the planning curriculum at the School of Planning, Ahmedabad, which Benninger founded in 1971. They were the basis for the new capital plan for Thimphu, Bhutan.

9.1.1 Principle one: a balance with nature

According to proponents of intelligent urbanism, balance with nature emphasizes the distinction between utilizing resources and exploiting them. It focuses on the thresholds beyond which deforestation, soil erosion, aquifer depletion, siltation and flooding reinforce one another in urban development, saving or destroying life support systems. The principle promotes environmental assessments to identify fragile zones, threatened ecosystems and habitats that can be enhanced through conservation, density control, land use planning and open space design. This principle promotes life cycle building energy consumption and pollutant emission analysis.

This principle states there is a level of human habitation intensity wherein the resources that are consumed will be replaced through the replenishing natural cycles of the seasons, creating environmental equilibrium. Embedded in the principle is contention that so long as nature can resurge each year; so long as the biomass can survive within its own eco-system; so long as the breeding grounds of fauna and avifauna are safe; so long as there is no erosion and the biomass is maintained, nature is only being utilized.

Underlying this principle is the supposition that there is a fragile line that is crossed when the fauna, which cross-fertilizes the flora, which sustains the soil, which supports the hillsides, is no longer there. After a point of no return, utilization of natural resources will outpace the natural ability of the eco-system to replenish itself. From there on degradation accelerates and amplifies. Deforestation, desertification, erosion, floods, fires and landslides all increase.

The principle states that blatant "acts against nature" include cutting of hillside trees, quarrying on slopes, dumping sewage and industrial waste into the natural drainage system, paving and plinthing excessively, and construction on steep slopes. This urban theory proposes that the urban ecological balance can be maintained when fragile areas are reserved, conservation of ecosystems is pursued, and low intensity habitation precincts are thoughtfully identified. Thus, the principles operate within the balance of nature, with a goal of protecting and conserving those elements of the ecology that nurture the environment. Therefore, the first principle of intelligent urbanism is that urbanization be in balance with nature.

9.1.2 Principle two: a balance with tradition

Balance with tradition is intended to integrate plan interventions with existing cultural assets, respecting traditional practices and precedents of style. This urban planning principle demands respect for the cultural heritage of a place. It seeks out traditional wisdom in the layout of human settlements, in the order of building plans, in the precedents of style, in the symbols and signs that transfer meanings through decoration and motifs. This principle respects the order engendered into building systems through years of adaptation to climate, to social circumstances, to available materials and to technology. It promotes architectural styles and motifs designed to communicate cultural values.

This principle calls for orienting attention toward historic monuments and heritage structures, leaving space at the ends of visual axis to "frame" existing views and vistas. Natural views and vistas demand respect, assuring that buildings do not block major sight lines toward visual assets.

Embedded in the principle is the concern for unique cultural and societal iconography of regions, their signs and symbols. Their incorporation into the spatial order of urban settings is promoted. Adherents promote the orientation and structuring of urban plans using local knowledge and meaning systems, expressed through art, urban space and architecture.

Planning decisions must operate within the balance of tradition, aggressively protecting, promoting and conserving generic components and elements of the urban pattern.

9.1.3 Principle three: appropriate technology

Appropriate technology emphasizes the employment of building materials, construction techniques, infrastructural systems and project management which are consistent with local contexts (situation, setting or circumstances). People's capacities, geo-climatic conditions, locally available resources, and suitable capital investments all temper technology. Where there are abundant craftspeople, labour-intensive methods are appropriate. Where there is surplus savings, capital intensive methods are appropriate. For every problem there is a range of potential technologies, which can be applied, and an appropriate fit between technology and other resources must be established. Proponents argue that accountability and transparency are enhanced by overlaying the physical spread of urban utilities and services upon electoral constituencies, such that people's representatives are interlinked with the urban technical systems needed for a civil society. This principle is in sync with "small is beautiful" concepts and with the use of local resources.

9.1.4 Principle four: conviviality

The fourth principle sponsors social interaction through public domains, in a hierarchy of places, devised for personal solace, companionship, romance, domesticity, "neighborliness," community and civic life (Jacobs:1993). According to proponents of intelligent urbanism, vibrant societies are interactive, socially engaging and offer their members numerous opportunities for gathering and meeting one another. The PIU maintain that this can be achieved through design and that society operates within hierarchies of social relations which are space specific. The hierarchies can be conceptualized as a system of social tiers, with each tier having a corresponding physical place in the settlement structure.

9.1.5 Principle five: efficiency

The principle of efficiency promotes a balance between the consumption of resources such as energy, time and fiscal resources, with planned achievements in comfort, safety, security, access, tenure, productivity and hygiene. It encourages optimum sharing of public land, roads, facilities, services and infrastructural networks, reducing per household costs, while increasing affordability, productivity, access and civic viability.

Intelligent urbanism promotes a balance between performance and consumption. Intelligent urbanism promotes efficiency in carrying out functions in a cost effective manner. It assesses the performance of various systems required by the public and the consumption of energy, funds, administrative time and the maintenance efforts required to perform these functions.

A major concern of this principle is transport. While recognizing the convenience of personal vehicles, it attempts to place costs (such as energy consumption, large paved areas, parking, accidents, negative balance of trade, pollution and related morbidity) on the users of private vehicles.

Good city planning practice promotes alternative modes of transport, as opposed to a dependence on personal vehicles. It promotes affordable public transport. It promotes medium to high-density residential development along with complementary social amenities, convenience shopping, recreation and public services in compact, walkable mixed-use settlements. These compact communities have shorter pipe lengths, wire lengths, cable lengths and road lengths per capita. More people share gardens, shops and transit stops.[4]

These compact urban nodes are spaced along regional urban transport corridors that integrate the region's urban nodes, through public transport, into a rational system of growth. Good planning practice promotes clean, comfortable, safe and speedy, public transport, which operates at dependable intervals along major origin and destination paths. Such a system is cheaper, safer, less polluting and consumes less energy.

The same principle applies to public infrastructure, social facilities and public services. Compact, high-density communities result in more efficient urban systems, delivering services at less cost per unit to each citizen.

There is an appropriate balance to be found somewhere on the line between wasteful low-density individual systems and over-capitalized mega systems. Individual septic tanks and water bores servicing individual households in low-density fragmented layouts, allow the use of filtered greywater for free irrigation of gardens, but, if not maintained, can cause a local pollution of subterranean aquifer systems. The bores can dramatically lower ground water levels especially during droughts. The vantage of septic tanks and bores is to be managed by the very users, at no cost for the community. Alternatively, large-scale, citywide sewerage systems and regional water supply systems are capital intensive and prone to management and maintenance dysfunction, if not corruption or extortion by private companies. Operating costs, user fees and cost recovery expenses are high. There is a balance wherein medium-scale systems, covering compact communities, utilize modern technology, without the pitfalls of large-scale infrastructure systems. This principle of urbanism promotes the middle path with regard to public infrastructure, facilities, services and amenities.

When these appropriate facilities and service systems overlap electoral constituencies, the "imagery" between user performance in the form of payments for services, systems dependability through managed delivery, and official response through effective representation, should all become obvious and transparent.

Good city planning practices promote compact settlements along dense urban corridors, and within populated networks, such that the numbers of users who share costs are adequate to support effective and efficient infrastructure systems. Intelligent urbanism is intended to foster movement on foot, linking pedestrian movement with public transport systems at strategic nodes and hubs. Medium-scale infrastructural systems, whose catchment areas overlap political constituencies and administrative jurisdictions, result in transparent governance and accountable urban management.

9.1.6 Principle six: human scale

Intelligent urbanism encourages ground level, pedestrian oriented urban patterns, based on anthropometric dimensions. Walkable, mixed use urban villages are encouraged over single-function blocks, linked by motor ways, and surrounded by parking lots.

An abiding axiom of urban planning, urban design and city planning has been the promotion of people friendly places, pedestrian walkways and public domains where people can meet freely. These can be parks, gardens, glass-covered gallerias, arcades, courtyards, street side cafes, river- and hill-side stroll ways, and a variety of semi-covered spaces.

Intelligent urbanism promotes the scale of the pedestrian moving on the pathway, as opposed to the scale of the automobile on the expressway. Intelligent urbanism promotes the ground plan of imaginable precincts, as opposed to the imagery of façades and the monumentality of the section. It promotes the personal visibility of places moving on foot at eye level.

Intelligent urbanism advocates removing artificial barrier and promotes face-to-face contact. Proponents argue that the automobile, single use zoning and the construction of public structures in isolated compounds, all deteriorate the human condition and the human scale of the city.

According to PIU proponents, the trend towards urban sprawl can be overcome by developing pedestrian circulation networks along streets and open spaces that link local destinations. Shops, amenities, day care, vegetable markets and basic social services should be clustered around public transport stops, and at a walkable distance from work places, public institutions, high and medium density residential areas. Public spaces should be integrated into residential, work, entertainment and commercial areas. Social activities and public buildings should orient onto public open spaces. These should be the interchange sites for people on the move, where they can also revert into the realm of "slowness," of community life and of human interaction.

Human scale can be achieved through building masses that "step down" to human scale open spaces; by using arcades and pavilions as buffers to large masses; by intermixing open spaces and built masses sensitively; by using anthropometric proportions and natural materials. Traditional building precedents often carry within them a human scale language, from which a contemporary fabric of build may evolve.

The focus of intelligent urbanism is the ground plane, pedestrian movement and interaction along movement channels, stems, at crossing nodes, at interactive hubs and within vibrant urban cores. The PIU holds many values in common with Transit Oriented Development, but the PIU goal is not merely to replace the automobile, nor to balance it. These are mundane requirements of planning, which the PIU assumes are found in every design and urban configuration. The PIU goal is to enrich the human condition and to enhance the realm of human possibilities.

Intelligent urbanism conceives of urbanity as a process of facilitating human behavior toward more tolerant, more peaceful, more accommodating and more sensitive modalities of interaction and conflict resolution. Intelligent urbanism recognizes that 'urbanity' emerges where people mix and interact on a face-to-face basis, on the ground, at high densities and amongst diverse social and economic groups. Intelligent urbanism nurtures 'urbanity' through designs and plans that foster human scale interaction.

9.1.7 Principle seven: opportunity matrix

The PIU envisions the city as a vehicle for personal, social, and economic development, through access to a range of organizations, services, facilities and information providing a variety of opportunities for enhanced employment, economic engagement, education, and recreation. This principle aims to increase access to shelter, health care and human resources development. It aims to increase safety and hygienic conditions. The city is a place of economic opportunity. This is generally said with regard to urban annual net product, enriched urban economic base, sustained employment generation and urban balance of trade. More significantly this is true for the individuals who settle in cities. Moreover, cities are places where individuals can increase their knowledge, skills and sensitivities. Cities provide access to health care and preventive medicine. They provide a great umbrella of services under which the individual can leave aside the struggle for survival, and get on with the finer things of life.

The PIU sees cities as catalysts for personal definition and self-discovery. In cities people get inspired, build a drive to achieve, discover aspects of their personalities, skills and intellectual curiosity which they use to craft their identity.

The city provides a range of services and facilities, whose realization in villages are the all-consuming struggle of rural inhabitants. Potable water; sewerage management; energy for cooking, heat and lighting are all piped and wired in; solid waste disposal and storm water drainage are taken for granted. The city offers access through roads, public transit, telephones and the Internet. The peace and security provided by effective policing systems, and the courts of law, are just assumed to be there in the city. Then there are the schools, the recreation facilities, the health services and a myriad of professional services offered in the city market place.

Intelligent urbanism views the city as an opportunity system. Yet these opportunities are not equally distributed. Security, health care, education, shelter, hygiene, and most of all employment, are not equally accessible. Proponents of intelligent urbanism see the city as playing an equalizing role allowing citizens to grow according to their own essential capabilities and efforts. If the city is an institution, which generates opportunities, intelligent urbanism promotes the concept of equal access to opportunities within the urban system.

Intelligent urbanism promotes a guaranteed access to education, health care, police protection, and justice before the law, potable water, and a range of basic services. Perhaps this principle, more than any other, distinguishes intelligent urbanism from other elitist, efficiency oriented urban charters and regimes.

Intelligent urbanism does not say every household will stay in an equivalent house, or travel in the same vehicle, or consume the same amount of electricity.

Intelligent urbanism recognizes the existence of poverty, of ignorance, of ill health, of malnutrition, of low skills, of gender bias and ignorance of the urban system itself. Intelligent urbanism is courageous in confronting these forms of inequality, and backlogs in social and economic development. Intelligent urbanism sees an urban plan, not only as a physical plan, but also as a social plan and as an economic plan.

The ramifications of this understanding are that the people living in intelligent cities should not experience urban development in "standard doses". In short, people may be born equal or unequal, but they grow inequitably. An important role of the city is to provide a variety of paths and channels for each individual to set right their own future, against the inequity of their past, or the special challenges they face. According to proponents of this principle this is the most salient aspect of a free society; than even voting rights access to opportunity is the essence of self-liberation and human development.

According to proponents of intelligent urbanism, there will be a variety of problems faced by urbanites and they need a variety of opportunity channels for resolution. If there are ten problem areas where people are facing stresses, like economic engagement, health, shelter, food, education, recreation, transport, etc., there must be a variety of opportunities through which individuals and households can resolve each of these stresses. There must be ten channels to resolve each of ten stresses! If this opportunity matrix is understood and responded to, the city is truly functioning as an opportunity matrix. For example, opportunities for shelter could be through the channels of lodges, rented rooms, studio apartments, bedroom apartments and houses. It could be through the channels of ownership, through a variety of tendencies. It could be through opportunities for self-help, or incremental housing. It could be through the up-gradation of slums. Intelligent urbanism promotes a wide range of solutions, where any stress is felt. It therefore promotes a range of problem statements, options, and variable solutions to urban stresses.

Intelligent urbanism sees cities as processes. Proponents argue that good urban plans facilitate those processes and do not place barriers before them. For example, it does not judge a "slum" as a blight on society; it sees the possibility that such a settlement may be an opportunity channel for entry into the city. Such a settlement may be the only affordable shelter, within easy access to employment and education, for a new immigrant household in the city. According to intelligent urbanism, if the plan ignores, or destroys such settlements, it is creating a city of barriers and despair wherein a poor family, offering a good service to the city, is denied a modicum of basic needs for survival. Alternatively, if the urban plan recognizes that the "slum" is a mechanism for self-development, a spring-board from which children have access to education, a place which can be up-graded with potable water, basic sanitary facilities, street lights and paving...then it is a plan for opportunity. Intelligent urbanism believes that there are slums of hope and slums of despair. It promotes slums of hope, which contribute, not only to individual opportunities, but also to nation building.

The opportunity matrix must also respond to young professionals, to skilled, well-paid day laborers, to the upper middle class and to affluent entrepreneurs. If a range of needs, of abilities to pay, of locational requirements, and of levels of development of shelter, is addressed, then opportunities are being created.

Intelligent urbanism believes that private enterprise is the logical provider of opportunities, but that alone it will not be just or effective. The regime of land, left to market forces alone, will create an exclusive, dysfunctional society.

Intelligent urbanism believes that there is an essential role for the civil society to intervene in the opportunity matrix of the city.

Intelligent urbanism promotes opportunities through access to:

- Basic and primary education, skill development and knowledge about the urban world;
- Basic health care, potable water, solid waste disposal and hygiene;
- Urban facilities like storm drainage, street lights, roads and footpaths;
- Recreation and entertainment;
- Transport, energy, communications;
- Public participation and debate;
- Finance and investment mechanisms;
- Land and/or built-up space where goods and services can be produced;
- Rudimentary economic infrastructure;
- Intelligent urbanism provides a wide range of zones, districts and precincts where activities and functions can occur without detracting from one another.

Intelligent urbanism proposes that enterprise can only flourish where a public framework provides opportunities for enterprise. This system of opportunities operates through public investments in economic and social infrastructure; through incentives in the form of appropriate finance, tax inducements, subsidized skill development for workers, and: regulations which protect the environment, safety, hygiene and health. To ensure a stable playing field where one can make an investment with predictable returns, a modicum of regulation is necessary. Proponents argue that it is through government regulations that private investment can be protected from fraud. It is through government regulation that the under-pinning conditions for free enterprise can be protected.

9.1.8 Principle eight: regional integration

Intelligent urbanism envisions the city as an organic part of a larger environmental, socio-economic and cultural-geographic system, essential for its sustainability. This zone of influence is the region. Likewise, it sees the region as integrally connected to the city. Intelligent urbanism sees the planning of the city and its hinterland as a single holistic process. Proponents argue if one does not recognize growth as a regional phenomenon, then development will play a hopscotch game of moving just a bit further along an arterial roads, further up valleys above the municipal jurisdiction, staying beyond the path of the city boundary, development regulations and of the urban tax regime.

The region may be defined as the catchment area from which employees and students commute into thc city on a daily basis. It is the catchment area from which people choose to visit one city, as opposed to another, for retail shopping and entertainment. Economically the city region may include the hinterland that depends on its wholesale markets, banking facilities, transport hubs and information exchanges. The region needing integration may be seen as the zone from which perishable foods, firewood and building materials supply the city. The economic region can also be defined as the area managed by exchanges in the city. Telephone calls to the region go through the city's telecom exchange; post goes through the city's general post office; money transfers go through the city's financial institutions and internet data passes electronically through the city's servers. The area over which "city exchanges" disperse matter can well be called the city's economic hinterland or region. Usually the region includes dormitory communities, airports, water reservoirs, perishable food farms, hydro facilities, out-of-doors recreation and other infrastructure that serves the city. Intelligent urbanism sees the integrated planning of these services and facilities as part of the city planning process.

Intelligent urbanism understands that the social and economic region linked to a city also has a physical form, or a geographic character. A hierarchy of watersheds, creating valleys and defining edges of neighborhoods, may define the geographic character. Forest ranges, fauna and avifauna habitats are set within such regions and are connected by natural corridors for movement and cross-fertilization. Within this larger, environmental scenario, one must conceptualize urbanism in terms of watersheds, subterranean aquifer systems, and other natural systems that operate across the entire region. Economic infrastructure, such as roads, hydro basins, irrigation channels, water reservoirs and related distribution networks usually follow the terrain of the regional geography. The region's geographic portals, and lines of control, may also define defense and security systems deployment.

Intelligent urbanism recognizes that there is always a spill over of population from the city into the region, and that population in the region moves into the city for work, shopping, entertainment, health care and education. With thoughtful planning the region can take pressure off of the city. Traditional and new settlements within the urban region can be enhanced and densified to accommodate additional urban households. There are many activities within the city, which are growing and are incompatible with urban habitat. Large, noisy and polluting workshops and manufacturing units are amongst these. Large wholesale markets, storage sheds, vehicular maintenance garages, and waste management facilities need to be housed outside of the city's limits in their own satellite enclaves. In larger urban agglomerations a number of towns and cities are clustered around a major urban center forming a metropolitan region.

Intelligent urbanism is not just planning for the present; it is also planning for the distant future. Intelligent urbanism is not Utopian, but futuristic in its need to forecast the scenarios to come, within its own boundaries, and within the boundaries of the distant future.

9.1.9 Principle nine: balanced movement

Intelligent urbanism advocates integrated transport systems comprising walkways, cycle paths, bus lanes, light rail corridors, under-ground metros and automobile channels. A balance between appropriate modes of movement is proposed. More capital intensive transport systems should move between high density nodes and hubs, which interchange with lower technology movement options. These modal split nodes become the public domains around which cluster high density, pedestrian, mixed-use urban villages.

The PIU accepts that the automobile is here to stay, but that it should not be made essential by design. A well planned metropolis would densify along mass transit corridors and around major urban hubs. Smaller, yet dense, urban nodes are seen as micro-zones of medium level density, public amenities and pedestrian access. At these points lower level nodal split will occur, such as between bus loops and cycle tracts. The PIU views nodal split points as places of urban conviviality and access to services and facilities. Modal split can be between walking, cycling, driving, and mass transit. Bus loops may feed larger rail-based rapid-movement corridors. Social and economic infrastructure becomes more intensive as movement corridors become more intense.

9.1.10 Principle ten: institutional integrity

Intelligent urbanism holds that good practices inherent in considered principles can only be realized through accountable, transparent, competent and participatory local governance, founded on appropriate data bases, due entitlements, civic responsibilities and duties. The PIU promotes a range of facilitative and promotive urban development management tools to achieve appropriate urban practices, systems and forms. None of the principles or practices the PIU promotes can be implemented unless there is a strong and rational institutional framework to define, channel and legalize urban development, in all of its aspects. Intelligent urbanism envisions the institutional framework as being very clear about the rules and regulations it sponsors and that those using discretion in implementing these measures must do so in a totally open, recorded and transparent manner.

Intelligent urbanism facilitates the public in carrying out their honest objectives. It does not regulate and control the public. It attempts to reduce the requirements, steps and documentation required for citizens to process their proposals.

Intelligent urbanism is also promotive in furthering the interests of the public in their genuine utilization of opportunities. It promotes site and services schemes for households who can construct their own houses. It promotes up-gradation of settlements with inadequate basic services. It promotes innovative financing to a range of actors who can contribute to the city's development. Intelligent urbanism promotes a limited role for government, for example in "packaging" large-scale urban development schemes, so that the private sector is promoted to actually build and market urban projects, which were previously built by the government.

Intelligent urbanism does not consider itself naïve. It recognizes that there are developers and promoters who have no long term commitment to their own constructions, and their only concern is to hand over a dwelling, gain their profit and move on. For these players it is essential to have Development Control Regulations, which assure the public that the products they invest in are safe, hygienic, orderly, durable and efficient. For the discerning citizen, such rules also lay out the civil understanding by which a complex society agrees to live together.

The PIU contends that there must be a cadastral System wherein all of the land in the jurisdiction of cities is demarcated, surveyed, characterized and archived, registering its legal owner, its legal uses, and the tax defaults against it.

The institutional framework can only operate where there is a Structure Plan, or other document that defines how the land will be used, serviced, and accessed. The Structure Plan tells landowners and promoters what the parameters of development are, which assures that their immediate investments are secure, and that the returns and use of such efforts are predictable. A Structure Plan is intended to provide owners and investors with predictable future scenarios. Cities require efficient patterns for their main infrastructure systems and utilities. According to PIU proponents, land needs to be used in a judicious manner, organizing complementary functions and activities into compact, mixed use precincts and separating out non-compatible uses into their own precincts. In a similar manner, proponents argue it is only through a plan that heritage sites and the environment can be legally protected. Public assets in the form of nature, religious places, heritage sites and open space systems must be designated in a legal plan.

Intelligent urbanism proposes that the city and its surrounding region be regulated by a Structure Plan, or equivalent mechanism, which acts as a legal instrument to guide the growth, development and enhancement of the city.

According to proponents, there must be a system of participation by the "Stake Holders" in the preparation of plans. Public meetings, hearings of objections and transparent processes of addressing objections, must be institutionalized. Intelligent urbanism promotes Public Participation. Local Area Plans must be prepared which address local issues and take into account local views and sentiments regarding plan objectives, configurations, standards and patterns. Such plans lay out the sites of plots showing the roads, public open spaces, amenities areas and conservation sites. Land Pooling assures the beneficiaries from provision of public infrastructure and amenities proportionally contribute and that a few individuals do not suffer from reservations in the plan.

According to proponents, there must be a system of Floor Area Ratios to assure that the land and the services are not over pressured. No single plot owner should have more than the determined "fair share" of utilization of the access roads, amenities and utilities that service all of the sites. Floor Area

Ratios temper this relationship as regulated the manner in which public services are consumed. According to PIU proponents, Transfer of Development Rights benefits land owners whose properties have been reserved under the plan. It also benefits the local authorities that lack the financial resources to purchase lands to implement the Structure Plans. It benefits concentrated, city center project promoters who have to amortize expensive land purchases, by allowing them to purchase the development rights from the owners of reserved lands and to hand over those properties to the plan implementing authority. This allows the local authority to widen roads and to implement the Structure Plan. The local authority then transfers the needed development right to city center promoters.

Intelligent urbanism supports the use of Architectural Guidelines where there is a tradition to preserve and where precedents can be used to specify architectural elements, motifs and language in a manner, which intended to reinforce a cultural tradition. Building designs must respect traditional elements, even though the components may vary greatly to integrate contemporary functions. Even in a Greenfield setting Architectural Guidelines are required to assure harmony and continuity of building proportions, scale, color, patterns, motifs, materials and facades.

Intelligent urbanism insists on safety, hygiene, durability and utility in the design and construction of buildings. Where large numbers of people gather in schools, hospitals, and other public facilities that may become emergency shelters in disasters, special care must be exercised. A suitable Building Code is the proposed instrument to achieve these aims.

PIU proponents state that those who design buildings must be professionally qualified architects; those who design the structures (especially of more than ground plus two levels) must be professionally qualified structural engineers; those who build buildings must be qualified civil engineers; and, those who supervise and control construction must be qualified construction managers. Intelligent urbanism promotes the professionalisation of the city making process. While promoting professionalism, intelligent urbanism proposes that this not become a barrier in the development process. Small structures, low-rise structures, and humble structures that do not house many people can be self-designed and constructed by the inhabitants themselves. Proponents maintain that there must be recognized Professional Accrediting Boards, or Professional Bodies, to see that urban development employs adequate technical competence.

Finally, there must be legislation creating statutory local authorities, and empowering them to act, manage, invest, service, protect, promote and facilitate urban development and all of the opportunities that a modern city must sponsor.

Intelligent urbanism insists that cities, local authorities, regional development commissions and planning agencies be professionally managed. City Managers can be hired to manage the delivery of services, the planning and management of planned development, the maintenance of utilities and the creation of amenities.

Intelligent urbanism views plans and urban designs and housing configurations as expressions of the people for whom they are planned. The processes of planning must therefore be a participatory involving a range of stakeholders. The process must be a transparent one, which makes those privileged to act as guardians of the people's will accountable for their decisions and choices. Intelligent urbanism sees urban planning and city governance as the most salient expressions of civility. Intelligent urbanism fosters the evolution of institutional systems that enhance transparency, accountability and rational public decision making.

9.2 Movements implementing the ten principles

Though not necessarily related to the principles of intelligent urbanism, there are examples representing all or some of them in urban design theory and practice. Concurrently, the recent movements of New Urbanism and New Classical Architecture promote a sustainable approach towards construction, that appreciates and develops smart growth, architectural tradition and classical design. This in contrast to modernist and globally uniform architecture, as well as leaning against solitary housing estates and suburban sprawl. Both trends started in the 1980s. The Driehaus Architecture Prize is an award that recognizes efforts in New Urbanism and New Classical Architecture, and is endowed with a prize money twice as high as that of the modernist Pritzker Prize.

10

SUSTAINABLE HEALTH & WELL BEING

Highlights:

- Focus on preventive measures
- Incentivizing healthy life-style
- Promotion of Natural Health care systems
- Integration of health with Education.

Sustainable health is a personal commitment to maintaining and taking responsibility for your own **health**, through preventative (proactive) means. This means not only having regular exercise, and taking care of what we eat, but also maintaining a **healthy** and balanced state of mind.

As the world is approaching a pandemic in obesity and stress related illnesses, such as high blood pressure, heart disease, cancer and diabetes, good health is something we take for granted. Most of us focus on our health, when we are ill or have had a major catastrophe in our lives, when it simply might be too late. Our society has conditioned us to constantly focus on our material wealth; at all costs however having good health is something money simply can't buy.

For 4,500 years, Indian Aryuvedic medicine has taught us that illnesses are caused through an unhealthy or unbalanced mind. Although modern science has disproved this, there is still some truth in the Aryuvedic approach. However, science just does not have all the answers and doesn't work for everyone. Health is a three way balance of genetics, environment and state of mind.

Most often genetics and environment are out of our control. Ultimately the only thing we can control is our state of mind and the toxins we put into it, through what we eat. If you take responsibility for your own health through preventative means, then ultimately you don't place a burden on the people you love such as your family, relatives and society in general. Taking care is the rule here.

Sustainable Health is:

- A preventative approach
- A balance of mind, body and spirit
- Taking care of what we put into our bodies
- Taking natural medicines to maintaining your health and hopefully preventing illnesses before they take shape.
- Leading and maintaining a balanced life, by taking a "middle road" approach. Not too little, not too much is the key. What are its aims?
- Taking responsible for one's own health, through a proactive approach rather than a reactive approach.

Current Approach

Most doctors fail to realize this because they and the industry work on reactive approach, and they are trained to think in a reactive approach. In western Sustainable Health civilization this is how doctors make a living and pharmaceutical companies thrive. Today we are ruled by pharmaceutical companies and health insurance companies, using a fear approach. Nearly all reactive medicines have side effects. Some have even been well documented by researchers and doctors.

Sustainable Health Principles

Your health is fundamentally directly related to your mental condition and toxins we put into our bodies, through what we eat, drink and breathe. Chronic and terminal illnesses doesn't just happen. They happen for a reason. A sure sign that you and your body may be out of balance or "sync" with your environment.

The 10 principles of Sustainable Health:

1. Maintain a balanced life, (middle road approach)
2. Have a healthy diet
3. Exercise regularly
4. Sleep well
5. Maintain a regular rhythm in life.
6. Take preventative natural medicines to maintain health
7. Engage in spiritual practices manifested through meditation, mind training and raising personal consciousness
8. Learn to live and laugh more

9. Building discipline in our selves through mind training and raising awareness
10. Take a simpler approach to life

The result of this will reduce your stress level and the impact of stress upon your health and body.

Balanced life

What is a balanced life? A balanced life means being in control of all aspects of our life, such as:

1. Physical
2. Mental
3. Spiritual
4. Family
5. Financial
6. Work and Career
7. Social

It also means not to live to excesses, because we become attached to them. When we become attached to them, we lose empowerment and they take over and control us. Point in example is TV, drugs and gambling.

Preventative Medicines

Tribal societies have long known about preventative, which we are only starting to realise now. Daily doses of preventative medicine may help you and boost yourimmune system. What are natural preventive medicines? Things like herbs, tonics, foods and drinks. Things like fresh fruit or plants like St.JohnsWort, Aloe Vera or Mangosteen, just to name a few.

Spiritual Practices

Why do we need to maintain a spiritual approach? What if I am an atheist or don't believe in God? Being spiritual doesn't necessary mean believing in God. Believing in oneself is far more important. In essence you have God within, but mostpeople fail to realize and acknowledge it.

Sleep

What is the importance of sleep? Why is it so beneficial?Hazrat Khan a famous Sufi teacher, lecturer, writer, and musician from India has described sleep as "food for the soul". Rumi another famous Sufi poet says in one of his poems, "O sleep, every night thou freest the prisoner from his bonds." "The prisoner when he is asleep does not know that he is in prison; he is free. The wretched is not wretched; he is contended. The suffering have no more pain and misery." 1•Sleep frees and rests our mind, and ultimately our soul.

Being happy

Studies have shown that happy people are also healthier people. Happiness is simply a state of mind. Being happy truly comes when we are in control of our own thoughts and actions. How can one be happy in the modern world with all the tragedies, violence and terrorism? One must remember that it's not what happens to us that counts (because most often it is out of our control), but how we deal with it. We can control how we react to it. We have a choice. The choice is to react to it in a negative way or positive way.

If we have a defeatist, negative attitude then we lose our empowerment. If we take a positive, courageous attitude, then we can be empowered. How is it that after the Boxing Day tsunami of 2004, children can still laugh and play and carry on with their day to day activities? The universe tells us that nature of life is to go on and the carrier of life is hope. Perhaps we can take a lesson from these unfortunate people, to free our minds up, because we often find that we are prisoners of our own devices attached to comforts and material possessions we don't really need driven by our insecurities and status anxiety. These insecurities are manifested through modern day media which is driven by society's capitalistic ideals.

Regular rhythm

What is so important about a regular rhythm? Life and nature works in natural cycles and natural rhythms. Our world tries to take that away from us, by distancing us from the natural cycles and creating artificial cycles, like for example night shift. If we were meant to live and work at night wouldn't we have larger eyes or special night vision like cats? Doesn't that make sense?

Simpler approach to life

A simpler approach to life doesn't mean, we all throw away everything and live like hermits in the bush or jungle. This is simply not a practical approach. What it does mean is removing ourselves from attachments and clutter.

Why would we want to remove ourselves from attachments? Don't attachments define who we are? The more attachments we have the more stress we induce upon ourselves, because having more attachments require more care and headaches. More headaches ultimately mean more stress.

More importantly the more attachments we have means the less we are empowered, which means we can feel helpless and be manipulated or controlled by larger external forces far more easily. Forces and entities like the media or government and authorities.

We ultimately become "prisoners of our own devices and remove ourselves from the true nature of being, distracted from the universe by things that matter very little in the grand scheme of things."

10.1 National Policy Framework for Sustainable Health (As recommended by the World Health Organisation)

There is no one-size-fits-all approach to integrating sustainability concerns into the operations and functions of health systems. Nonetheless, regardless of the specific context, there is value in adopting a formal national policy framework, developed through a consultative process involving health workers and other major stakeholders.

This national policy would be best accompanied by a strategy or action plan including measurable performance objectives and clear roles and responsibilities to ensure transparency, accountability and effective partnerships.

Common elements of this policy are described below, including key actions that could help in that process.

10.1.1 Minimizing and adequately managing waste and hazardous chemicals

The issues of health-care waste and the use and disposal of hazardous chemicals in health systems are highly related.

Health-care waste includes general waste that is comparable to domestic waste; infectious waste such as pathological waste; sharps, chemicals; pharmaceuticals; genotoxic waste; radioactive waste; and heavy metals such as broken mercury thermometers (WHO, 2015a; GuardinoSolá, 2011).

Poor management of health-care waste exposes health care workers, waste handlers and the community to infections, toxic effects, injuries, and poisoning and pollution by toxic elements or compounds such as mercury or dioxins that are released during incineration (Chartier et al., 2014). If properly segregated, much of health care facilities' general waste stream can be recycled.

In addition, a number of the products used in health services (for example, cleaners, disinfectants, some medical devices, electronic equipment, etc.) contain hazardous chemicals that can cause occupational risks as well as downstream health impacts through pollution and inadequate disposal. This is linked with the issue of waste management in health systems.

Possible actions include:

1) ensuring adequate management of health-care waste and promoting the minimization of general non-hazardous waste; and
2) minimizing the use of products containing hazardous chemicals in health systems. This can be done by:

* developing and implementing measures to manage and minimize the production of health-care waste in line with the recommendations of the WHO guidance handbook Safe management of wastes from health-care activities (Chartier et al., 2014);

- minimizing the production of general nonhazardous waste through adequate classification, waste reduction, reuse and recycling;
- developing a chemicals policy in health systems in accordance with local, national and supranational regulations;
- prioritizing chemicals for minimization and substitution based on scientific and economic evidence;
- and where medically, technically and economically feasible, substituting products containing hazardous chemicals for less hazardous alternatives within health systems.

10.1.2 Promoting an efficient management of resources

Safe water, sanitation and hygiene (WASH), buildings, and energy are all essential components of basic health services provision. Large efficiency gains can be achieved by adequately managing the use of such basic resources in health systems, specifically health care facilities and utilities.

Evidence from a wide variety of countries illustrates the potential for resource and cost savings based on conscious, data-driven health care facility management.

Possible actions include encouraging efficiency in the design, operation and maintenance of facilities and systems, and in the use of resources. Below are examples from the areas of WASH, buildings and energy.

WASH. Developing and implementing water safety plans is an effective means to provide safe drinking-water for common domestic uses in health care facilities (for example, hydration, personal hygiene, food preparation) as well as care-related uses. These plans should place specific emphasis on the needs and requirements of different patient groups (Adams, Bartram &Chartier, 2008; Cunliffe et al., 2011).

Reducing water usage in health care facilities contributes to conservation of local water sources and to health systems resilience, especially in water-stressed regions, and is possible through various interventions (for example, installation of water-saving armatures and devices).

Safe management and disposal of wastewater and/or human waste by health care facilities is essential for protecting patients, staff, communities and the environment. Moreover, since poor WASH can cause outbreaks and thereby lead to high demand on health services, engaging in broader advocacy for safe WASH – in the facility and the community – is in the interest of health systems' sustainability and resilience (to climate change and extreme events).

Buildings. Environmental sustainability considerations can be incorporated during the design, construction and/or rehabilitation of buildings housing health care facilities. In the design phase, harmful pollution and carbon emissions from the extraction of raw materials can be minimized. Improving elements of building planning and design such as site location, artificial lighting, natural ventilation, and open and green spaces can also minimize environmental impacts, improve patient experience (for example, thermal comfort) and increase resilience to the projected impacts of climate change. Throughout the lifetime of a building, efficiency measures can include improved insulation, the use of natural ventilation, energy-efficient lighting or the installation of combined heat and power systems. In the rehabilitation of buildings, eliminating harmful substances is an important aspect.

Energy. Three main principles can help guide action related to the use of energy within health systems: 1) reducing unnecessary usage, 2) increasing energy efficiency, and 3) understanding where energy supply resilience can be improved. Benefits include improved security of energy supply for operating theatres and incubators, providing hot water and improved medicines, and refrigerating vaccines, as well as decreased emissions of air pollutants with associated advantages for the health of the population. In turn, improved energy security increases health systems resilience. Any energy savings, however, must not compromise patient and staff safety. For example, to minimize risks of Legionella infections in health-care facilities, water temperatures of above 50 °C in hot water systems need to be maintained. Lowering the hot water temperature in favour of saving energy may compromise patient and worker safety.

10.1.3 Promoting sustainable procurement

Health systems procure and use significant amounts of goods and services which can have effects on the environment throughout their life cycle – from the initial extraction of raw materials to their manufacture, transport, use and disposal. In fact, evidence suggests that most of the operational environmental footprint of health systems is related to procured goods and services.

Possible actions to encouraging sustainable procurement include:

- using health systems' buying power to maximize positive environmental outcomes, recognizing that influencing suppliers to factor environmental impacts into their manufacturing processes is a powerful lever for significant change;

- reducing demand by looking for opportunities to buy and use less, constantly questioning whether procured products are necessary, supporting interventions that reduce demand for products or use them more efficiently, and ensuring that procured products are not wasted;
- increasing efficiency by buying products, equipment or services that consume less and have a lower environmental impact during their in-use life and at disposal; and
- assessing the environmental impact of products and services used or delivered by the health system and, where appropriate, substituting or innovating with alternative products, materials or approaches that have less impact on the environment and are more sustainable.

10.1.4 Reducing health systems' emissions of greenhouse gases and air pollution

Health systems as a whole are carbon intensive, thus contributing to climate change. In turn, health effects from climate change will continue to add pressure to health systems through an increase in the overall burden of disease. World Health Assembly resolution WHA68.8 urges health systems to address air pollution comprehensively: 1) with a cross-sectoral, health-in-all-policies approach, and 2) by minimizing "as far as possible air pollution specifically associated with health care activities, including by implementing, as appropriate, relevant WHO guidelines" (WHA, 2015). Health systems face an opportunity to lead by example in this area, and to promote reduction in emission of air pollutants and greenhouse gasses from a health standpoint.

Possible actions to reduce health systems' emissions include:

- developing and implementing an action plan for reducing emissions of air pollutants and greenhouse gases, informed by periodic carbon and pollution accounting exercises;
- promoting policies and interventions in all relevant areas that simultaneously reduce air pollution emissions and exposure as well as greenhouse gas emissions through a cross-sectoral, health-in-all-policies approach;
- prioritizing low-carbon alternatives in the design and operation of the built environment, procurement and purchasing, energy efficiency, energy sourcing, retrofitting and equipment; and
- promoting low-carbon alternatives in ancillary areas to health systems, such as non-motorized and/or public transportation, administration services, etc.

10.1.5 Prioritizing disease prevention, health promotion and public health services

Preventive approaches are cost-effective ways to reduce morbidity and premature mortality, and can contribute to wider sustainability with economic, social and environmental benefits (Merkur, Sassi & McDaid, 2013; WHO Regional Office for Europe, 2015a). Furthermore, scaling up inter-sectoral action on environmental sustainability and public health services can reduce negative health outcomes at their source (WHO

Regional Office for Europe, 2012a, 2012b) and facilitate earlier, more effective responses to environmental and climate-related risks. Healthcentred policies and programmes in sectors such as agriculture, transport, housing, and energy can lead to reduced environmental and health risks and improved health practices, behaviours and processes.

Possible actions to strengthen health protection and promotion services include:

- taking inter-sectoral action, providing evidence and raising awareness of environment and health aspects, and engaging in joint monitoring of environmental exposures and health outcomes;
- developing the institutional capacity for disease prevention, health promotion and public health services;
- strengthening monitoring compliance with environmental norms, regulations and standards; and
- further improving the performance of and access to environmental and occupational health services, promoting healthy environments (including healthy workplaces), safe and healthy foods, good air quality, and supply chain safety and security.

10.1.6 Engaging the health workforce as an agent of sustainability

Efforts to strengthen environmental sustainability in health systems can succeed only with the active collaboration of an engaged health workforce. By engaging health workers in the process of creating, implementing and managing the environmental sustainability policy, organizations in the health system can foster a sense of ownership in and responsibility for the policy's success.

Health workers will be far more likely to be successful in their efforts to foster sustainability if an empowering institutional environment is put in place through the adoption of a sustainability policy and strong support from executive management.

Possible actions to facilitate the leadership of health workers in environmental sustainability include:

- engaging the health workforce and its associations and unions in embedding environmental sustainability and resilience into health system culture through clear policies, capacity-building and motivation;
- educating the health workforce about the environmental impact of health systems;
- ensuring that staff development and performance-management processes support a shift to more environmentally sustainable and resilient health care;
- ensuring the health workforce is prepared and able to adapt to the projected impacts of climate change;
- ensuring the health workforce is protected from environmental hazards and that health is promoted in the workplace; and
- preparing the health workforce for environmental emergencies, and different environmental conditions (e.g. a changing climate).

10.1.7 Increasing community resilience and promoting local assets

The location and surroundings of health services entail both responsibilities and opportunities tied to the local context. On one hand, health systems can strengthen local assets and foster their own resilience and the community's; on the other, health systems' managers and workforces have a responsibility to promote environmental sustainability locally.

Possible actions to strengthen local assets, community resilience and environmental sustainability include:

- promoting environmentally sustainable actions that increase health systems' resilience to climate change, such as those fostering energy and water security, zoning regulations for health facilities, etc.;
- promoting and enabling the use of public transportation and non-motorized transportation (cycling and walking) for patients, visitors and staff;
- using local green spaces for health promotion activities and, where feasible and appropriate, other selected health systems activities (for example, nature-based therapy);
- ensuring that the planning and design phases for the construction of new health infrastructure consider areas that provide staff, visitors, patients and suppliers with good access via public transportation and active mobility, as well as appropriate facilities (for example, safe parking spaces, changing rooms and green spaces);
- sourcing food and other goods and services locally, where feasible and appropriate; and

- informing local communities about health systems activities and opportunities for involvement in health promotion activities and others where appropriate.

10.1.8 Creating incentives for change

The uptake and implementation of policies and efforts towards greater environmental sustainability in health systems are unlikely to succeed without the right structure of incentives in place.

While there are inherent incentives to greater environmental sustainability (for example, cost reductions), an adequate regulatory and institutional environment is needed to make them effective. Health authorities and regulators can devise additional incentives for the uptake and mainstreaming of environmental sustainability. These can be tangible or intangible, financial or otherwise.

Possible actions to contribute to or advocate for the creation of an incentive structure conducive to the uptake of environmental sustainability actions in health systems include:

- achieving cost savings through reduced consumption of energy and other resources that can be reinvested in core health-system functions;
- providing low-interest financing for projects enhancing environmental sustainability;
- implementing selected tax incentives linked to environmentally sustainable investments, etc.;
- making seed funding, additional funding or grants available for environmental sustainability initiatives; and

- creating reputational/image-based incentives, such as those from sustainability certifications and awards for institutions and professionals, or sustainability-related objectives in performance management schemes.

10.1.9 Promoting innovative models of care

Besides their crucial potential for benefitting patients, practitioners and health systems at large, innovative models of care have great potential to deliver benefits in terms of environmental sustainability. Conversely, interventions towards greater environmental sustainability may help strengthen the overall sustainability of innovative models of care; this becomes clear as more and better estimates of the potential health and environmental benefits of innovative models of care become available (Weisz et al., 2011).

Possible actions to encourage innovative models of care – once their health benefits for patients and operational benefits for practitioners are clear – include:

- changing emphasis and improving coordination between primary, secondary and tertiary levels of care;
- encouraging the use of innovative technologies, including telemedicine, e-health and mobile health; and
- changing clinical guidelines/standard operating procedures to reflect environmental sustainability.

11

SUSTAINABLE FOOD SYSTEM

Highlights:

- Based on Plants - Vegetables and Fruits
- Implementation of Food security measures
- Zero wastage of food
- Food without hazardous pesticides and chemicals, non-essential antibiotics

A **sustainable food system** is a type of food system that provides healthy food to people while also providing sustainable impacts on environmental, economic and social systems that surround food.

Sustainable food systems start with the development of sustainable agricultural practices, development of more sustainable food distribution systems, creation of sustainable diets and reduction of food waste throughout the system. Sustainable food systems have been argued to be central to manyor all17 Sustainable Development Goals.

Moving to sustainable food systems is an important component of addressing the causes of climate change. A

2020 review conducted for the European Union found that up to 37% of global greenhouse gas emissions could be attributed to the food system, including crop and livestock production, transportation, changing land use (including deforestation) and food loss and waste. Sustainable food systems are frequently at the center of sustainability focused policy programs..

11.1 Definition of Sustainable Food System

There are many different definitions of a sustainable food system.

From a global perspective, the Food and Agriculture Organization of the United Nations describes a sustainable food system as follows:

A sustainable food system (SFS) is a food system that delivers food security and nutrition for all in such a way that the economic, social and environmental bases to generate food security and nutrition for future generations are not compromised. This means that:

- It is profitable throughout (economic sustainability);
- It has broad-based benefits for society (social sustainability); and
- It has a positive or neutral impact on the natural environment (environmental sustainability)

The American Public Health Association (APHA) defines a sustainable food system as: one that provides healthy food to meet current food needs while maintaining healthy ecosystems that can also provide food for generations to come with minimal negative impact to the environment.

A sustainable food system also encourages local production and distribution infrastructures and makes nutritious food available, accessible, and affordable to all. Further, it is humane and just, protecting farmers and other workers, consumers, and communities

The European Union's Scientific Advice Mechanism defines a sustainable food system as a system that:

provides and promotes safe, nutritious and healthy food of low environmental impact for all current and future EU citizens in a manner that itself also protects and restores the natural environment and its ecosystem services, is robust and resilient, economically dynamic, just and fair, and socially acceptable and inclusive. It does so without compromising the availability of nutritious and healthy food for people living outside the EU, nor impairing their natural environment

In September 2019, the European Union's Chief Scientific Advisors stated that transitioning to a sustainable food system should be a high priority for the EU.

Although availability of food is not perceived as an immediate, major concern in Europe, the challenge to ensure a long-term, safe, nutritious and affordable supply of food, from both land and the oceans, remains. A portfolio of coordinated strategies is called for to address this challenge.

In January 2020, the EU put the transition to a sustainable food system at the core of the European Green Deal. The European Commission's 'Farm to Fork strategy for a sustainable food system', due to be published in spring 2020, is expected to lay out how European countries will reduce greenhouse gas emissions, protect biodiversity, reduce food waste and chemical pesticide use, and contribute to a circular economy.

In April 2020, the EU's Scientific Advice Mechanism delivered to European Commissioners a Scientific Opinion on how to transition to a sustainable food system, informed by an evidence review report undertaken by European academies.[

11.2 Problems with conventional food systems

Industrial agriculture causes environmental impacts, as well as health problems associated with obesity in the rich world and hunger in the poor world. This has generated a strong movement towards healthy, sustainable eating as a major component of overall ethical consumerism.

Conventional food systems are largely based on the availability of inexpensive fossil fuels, which is necessary for mechanized agriculture, the manufacture or collection of chemical fertilizers, the processing of food products, and the packaging of foods. Food processing began when the number of consumers started growing rapidly. The demand for cheap and efficient calories climbed resulting in nutrition decline. Industrialized agriculture, due to its reliance on economies of scale to reduce production costs, often leads to the compromising of local, regional, or even global ecosystems through fertilizer runoff, nonpoint source pollution, and greenhouse gas emission.

Also, the need to reduce production costs in an increasingly global market can cause production of foods to be moved to areas where economic costs (labor, taxes, etc.) are lower or environmental regulations are more lax, which are usually further from consumer markets.

For example, the majority of salmon sold in the United States is raised off the coast of Chile, due in large part to less stringent Chilean standards regarding fish feed and regardless of the fact that salmon are not indigenous in Chilean coastal waters. The globalization of food production can result in the loss of traditional food systems in less developed countries, and have negative impacts on the population health, ecosystems, and cultures in those countries.

11.3 Sourcing sustainable food

At the global level the environmental impact of agribusiness is being addressed through sustainable agriculture and organic farming. At the local level there are various movements working towards local food production, more productive use of urban wastelands and domestic gardens including permaculture, urban horticulture, local food, slow food, sustainable gardening, and organic gardening.

Sustainable seafood is seafood from either fished or farmed sources that can maintain or increase production in the future without jeopardizing the ecosystems from which it was acquired. The sustainable seafood movement has gained momentum as more people become aware about both overfishing and environmentally destructive fishing methods.

11.4 Local food systems

A local food system is one that shortens the distance between food producers and consumers, both literally and figuratively. In recent years, as consumers have become more interested in local food, markets have developed for direct-to-consumer sales, and also for institutional sales. But there are challenges involved in bringing local food back to scale.

"Local" is generally understood to mean products that are grown and processed relatively nearby to where they are sold, purchased and consumed.

The local food trend took off and got established through direct-to-consumer markets such as farmers' markets and community supported agriculture programs. As demand for local food has risen, additional marketing systems have been developed to scale up regional food systems and make these products available to more people.

11.5 Food distribution

Food distribution is a process in which a general population is supplied with food. The Food and Agriculture Organization (FAO) considers food distribution as a subset of the food system. The process and methodology behind food distribution varies by location. Food distribution has been a defining characteristic of human behavior in all societies, and recordings of food distribution date back for thousands of years. Most governments and societies are highly shaped by the systems created to support food distribution.

There are a multitude of risk factors that can affect food distribution. War, economic failure, political problems, and weather conditions all play a role in determining the efficiency of any food system. Two recent examples of war and economic failure impacting food distribution includes the decline of food distribution in Japan during World War II and food recession in Sub-Saharan Africa during the late 1970s and early 1980s. In both cases, food distribution was hindered and the population in these areas consequently suffered.

Special organizations exist today to prevent any total collapses in food distribution, assist in developing food distribution and food systems in underdeveloped areas, and respond to food distribution crises. At the international level, the Food and Agriculture Organization (FAO) plays a key role in facilitating the growth of food distribution systems all over the world. At the national level different countries have developed more complex support systems; by example, a mixture of federal, non-profit, and volunteer organizations function in the United States to safeguard the well-being of the US food distribution system.

11.6 Food security, nutrition and diet

The environmental effects of different dietary patterns depend on many factors, including the proportion of animal and plant foods consumed and the method of food production At the same time, current and future food systems need to be provide sufficient nutrition for not only the current population, but future population growth in light of a world effected by changing climate in the face of global warming.

11.7 Food waste

According to the Food and Agriculture Organization (FAO), food waste is responsible for 8 percent of global human-made greenhouse gas emissions. The FAO concludes that nearly 30 percent of all available agricultural land in the world - 1.4 billion hectares - is used for produced but uneaten food. The global blue water footprint of food waste is 250 km^3,that is the amount of water that flows annually through the Volga or 3 times Lake Geneva.

11.8 Factors of Food Sustainability

There is no one truth when it comes to defining food sustainability. Although most definitions cover the following factors:

11.8.1Sustainable Farming Practices

Food production needs to be profitable. Otherwise, farmers and producers would go out of business. But this doesn't have to mean mass scale food production that's bad news for animals and the environment.

Sustainable farming aims to maintain or increase output, while increasing the environmental benefits.

Such farming requires an understanding of the surrounding ecosystem. This means it will protect the diversity of our native plants and animals while meeting the needs of the farm and its production system.

Farming that aims to be sustainable has to protect biodiversity. It has to be beneficial to plants, animals and the environment. Sustainable farming also has to protect soil fertility for future food production.

Thankfully an increased number of farms and farmers are moving to more sustainable farming practices.

Sustainable agriculture supports organic and low carbon food production. It also avoids the use of artificial fertilisers and pesticides as well as genetically modified organisms.

Farms that are sustainable also make use of better farming practices.. These include crop rotation and avoiding the use of monocrops.

Planting varied crops helps with soil fertility and biodiversity. They also tend to manage pests with natural predators, plow their fields less and integrate crops and livestock.

11.8.2 Low Environmental Impact

Sustainable food aims to avoid damaging or wasting natural resources. It also minimises its contribution to climate change throughout the whole production process.

The use of the earth's finite resources is also considered. This includes the use of energy in transportation and storage.

The impact on the surrounding flora and fauna, waterways, air and sound quality is also considered. Ideally any negative impact is minimised while aiming to produce food in the most efficient and cost effective way possible.

11.8.3 Upholding Animal Welfare

Sustainable farmers use livestock husbandry techniques that protect the animals' health and wellbeing.

They provide pasture grazing and allow animals to move freely. No animal is confined to a cage or restricted holding pens. This all ensures that animals are treated with care and respect.

Such farmers also aim to reduce, if not remove, the pain and suffering that animals may be subject to as part of the food production process.

11.8.4 Protection of Public Health

Sustainable food is food that is safe and healthy. It's produced without hazardous pesticides and chemicals, non-essential antibiotics or growth promotion supplements.

Nutrition is also playing an increasing role in defining sustainable foods. There's a growing movement towards plant-based foods. These foods tend to have a greater emphasis on whole foods and fewer processed ingredients.

11.8.5 Good Employment Practices and Community Support

Sustainable food brands pay workers a living wage alongside safe, hygienic and fair working conditions.

They support local and regional economies that offer jobs and build stronger communities.

11.9 How to Make Sustainable Food Choices?

As we walk the supermarket aisles, we're usually looking for our favourite products and culinary inspiration. Food sustainability isn't often at the forefront of our minds. Our decisions are based on convenience, taste and price. Even for those of us who wish to live more planet-friendly lives.

Having a better understanding of what makes a food sustainable could help us all make more informed decisions. It would allow us to weigh up products and brands more easily.

We could answer our "does this align with my values" questions more quickly. And we could consume more mindfully.

All this might seem daunting, but as with anything, learning and changing slowly is key. We don't have to completely rethink our shopping list.

Instead, we can make one or two changes each week or month. We can swap beef mince for veggie mince, choose fair trade coffee or have a go at reducing food waste at home.

Educating ourselves is important too. Becoming a regular reader of sites like ours will help. Knowing what is and what isn't sustainable is the first step to leading a more sustainable lifestyle. The second step is using that knowledge to make more informed choices.

There are many ways that you can choose to eat and live more sustainably:

1. Reduce the amount of meat, fish and dairy you eat. Animal agriculture is an industry with one of the largest carbon footprints. You don't have to go full on vegan, just reduce the amount of meat and dairy you eat and up the veggies!
2. Eating less meat and dairy means that you could spend a little extra on sustainably reared produce.
3. Choose to eat foods that are in season. Seasonal foods haven't had to be artificially ripened and are less likely to have come from overseas.
4. Likewise, foods that have been produced locally have fewer air miles.
5. Reduce your food waste. Because why would you want to waste all that consciously produced food?!
6. Reduce the amount of plastic that you use. Plastic only adds to the problems of sustainability as it's so energy intensive to make and recycle.
7. Choose products that have been traded fairly.
8. Grow your own herbs, fruit and vegetables. That way, you'll know exactly what's gone into producing them!
9. Support our native wildlife and plant life, plant a bee friendly garden.

11.10 Promotion of Circular Food System

Modern industrial food, energy and water systems are fundamentally unsustainable. Their linear, and increasingly globalised, structure assumes that the Earth has an endless supply of natural resources at one end, and a limitless capacity to absorb waste and pollution at the other. Our continued reliance on these industrial systems is pushing the world into a vicious cycle of food shortages, climate chaos, famine and disaster.

How can we transform our production models for food, energy and water to deliver lower ecological and social footprints? The answer lies in using circular models that mimic natural systems to reduce both external inputs and waste. Case studies from across the world show that circular production systems can and do work for sustainability and equity. But these remain largely isolated examples. Upscaling successful circular systems for food, energy, water and waste management requires policymakers to act on seven fronts.

11.10.1 Policy pointers

Equity and sustainability goals can be achieved by shifting from linear and globalised systems towards locally controlled circular systems that re-integrate and re-localise food and energy production with water and waste management.

Circular systems that mimic natural ecosystems can be developed at different scales, from individual farm plots to entire cities, by using functional biodiversity, ecological clustering of industries, recycling and re-localised production.

Well-designed circular systems can: reduce fossil fuel use and emissions; increase food, water and energy security;

create jobs; boost incomes; promote resilient and self-reliant communities; and enhance direct democracy

In most countries food, energy, waste and water management systems still rely heavily on industrial models or unsustainable resource use. Replicating sustainable circular systems on a much wider scale is now a key priority and challenge for today's decision makers and wider society.It is essential that organised citizens and policymakers across the world simultaneously redirect investments towards integrated, resilient and locally controlled circular models, and remove key obstacles limiting the spread of these systems in rural and urban areas.

Achieving these two goals in practice requires action on seven fronts.

1. Strengthening local organisations.

Individually and collectively, local organisations play a key role in: sustaining the ecosystems that underpin circular systems; coordinating human skills, knowledge and labour to generate economic wealth and exchanges in these multifunctional circular systems; and supporting the local governance of circular systems. Strengthening local organisations can help deliver cheaper, and more sustainable, solutions for farming and food processing, storage and distribution as well as for decentralised energy production, and water and waste management.

2. Promoting equitable access to resources

In the face of the widespread acquisition of land and water rights alongside the privatisation of seeds, alternative policies are needed to ensure equitable access, use and control over natural resources in rural and urban areas. Secure tenure rights play a vital role in spreading agroecological innovations and resilient circular economy models. Decision makers must abandon investment policies that favour land acquisitions and instead focus on strengthening customary tenure systems and removing discriminatory components against women.

3. Redistributing public goods

Integrated circular systems require investment in public goods such as infrastructure, accessible credit and training. Dedicated funds are also needed to support the supply of local inputs — including organic manure and composting units — and local food processing facilities, such as abattoirs, solar dryers or flour mills, alongside equipment that enables decentralised renewable energy provision and water recycling and purification.

4. Transforming research and development

Investments in research and development must focus on building and up-scaling decentralised food, energy, water and waste management systems based on circular economy models and local democratic control. This means that policies should encourage participatory research and training that emphasises the knowledge, skills and values needed to recycle, reuse and reduce resource consumption. Training centres should aim to strengthen local knowledge systems, organisations and institutions, thereby enhancing capacities for local innovation and their horizontal spread to more people and places.

5. Changing trade and market rules

Farmers and other citizens need enabling economic institutions — not only to produce food and energy but also to market their surpluses. In today's world, locally produced food, energy and clean water struggle to compete with subsidised imports. Policymakers urgently need to introduce trade rules and supply management policies that protect the local economy, strengthen self-managed cooperatives and local businesses, and provide incentives for local food and energy production.

Feed-in tariffs and internal markets can encourage decentralised micro-generation of renewable energies. Similarly, the spread of resilient food systems depends on: moving away from patents on biodiversity and other proprietary technologies towards legal frameworks that recognise farmers' rights and collective innovations; replacing uniform food safety standards with a diverse range of locally evolved and managed standards; and introducing local food, energy and water procurement schemes.

6. Penalising financial speculations and negative social or environmental impacts

The use of fiscal measures such as tax incentives and reforms can encourage the shift to sustainable circular systems. Relatively small taxes on financial speculations and other global money transactions should be introduced through a multilateral agreement that recognises the need for strong citizen oversight. This decision alone would generate immediate and substantial funding for the design and spread of circular systems that regenerate local ecologies and economies for the public good.

Policymakers should also introduce stricter, and more equitable, measures to internalise the environmental and social costs associated with the food, energy, water and transport systems that, for the most part, are controlled by large corporations. Resulting revenues should be used to support sustainable locally controlled initiatives and their federation from the ground up to enhance democracy and socio-ecological resilience at regional, national and global scales.

7. Upholding citizen rights to participate in policymaking

Governments have an obligation to support citizens' fundamental human right to participate in shaping the policies that affect them. More direct forms of democracy and much greater citizen engagement in framing policies and institutional choices can be encouraged by simultaneously strengthening civil society, encouraging deliberative and inclusive policy processes, expanding information democracy, nurturing active forms of citizenship, and learning from the rich history of direct democracy.

Policies also need to facilitate legal redress against abuses — not least because citizen participation increasingly takes place against a backdrop of transnational corporations and investors engaging in international arbitration to protect their rights as investors. For the first time in international law, large corporations are being given the right to sue governments. Citizens require safeguards against such abuses of power.